The Connecticut Historical Society
1825-1975

Reverend Thomas Robbins (1777–1856), charter member and first Librarian of The Connecticut Historical Society, as painted by Jared Bradley Flagg in 1847

The Connecticut Historical Society

1825-1975

A Brief Illustrated History

CHRISTOPHER P. BICKFORD

THE CONNECTICUT HISTORICAL SOCIETY
1975

Library of Congress Catalog Card Number: 75–11020

Bickford, Christopher P.
    The Connecticut Historical Society 1825–1975:
  A Brief Illustrated History
Connecticut   Connecticut Printers, Inc.
May 1975   3-29-75

Table of Contents

The Connecticut Historical Society
1825-1975

Introduction

IT WAS TWO GENERATIONS after the outbreak of the American Revolution—50 years and a few weeks, in fact—that The Connecticut Historical Society was established by State charter. One member of the Society—its first President, John Trumbull —had been able, through his anti-Tory verse, to advance the cause of independence. The rest of the 31 charter members of the Society in 1825 either had been too young to have served or had not yet been born. Most, however, had grown up in Connecticut families that had participated in the struggle for self-determination. In their maturity they had reaped the advantages of the freedoms secured through the Revolution, but they were disturbed by the apparent indifference to what they considered the manifest lessons of history. They shared the conviction that the heroic deeds of the colonial and revolutionary eras should be remembered; and they were in agreement that the manuscripts and printed records of those periods, the materials on which future generations would rely for their knowledge, should not be lost. As we approach the nation's second Centennial and pause to take stock of our collective past, it is appropriate to recall that The Connecticut Historical Society was founded to keep the consciousness of the past alive. In May of 1975, The Connecticut Historical Society will have completed its 150th year in the service of that goal.

The course of the Society's progress has not always run smoothly. As with other privately supported New England historical societies, initiative and financing rests entirely with committed individuals. There have been periods, notably from 1825 to 1839 and in the late nineteenth century, when interest slackened and its effectiveness declined. Understandably, the most dynamic years have coincided with the involvement of energetic people. The recent history of the Society is most encouraging. Today, with an active membership over 2,000, with a Director and supporting professional staff of eight, a substantial endowment and a modern building, The Connecticut Historical Society is fulfilling its purposes with unprecedented support, clarity and knowledge.

As with any institutional history, the story of The Connecticut Historical Society is one of change and continuity. The goals of 1825, the collection and preservation of the materials of United States and Connecticut history, have been periodically revised. The original purposes of the Society were influenced by two types of institutions: New England historical societies in existence in 1825 and literary and philosophical societies founded in the previous decades. Along with the preservation of historical materials, the Historical Society in 1825 also committed itself to the collection of current economic statistics and demographic facts. An interest in natural history lasted throughout the nineteenth century, partly because of the broad aims enunciated in 1825 and partly because of the absence in Hartford of a museum for the display of scientific exhibits and specimens. In recent years, the Society has come to concentrate exclusively on the sources of Connecticut history, conceding to other institutions the task of building collections of national scope. The Connecticut Historical Society has become increasingly selective in its acquisitions, depositing with other societies objects incompatible with its purposes. Yet continuity is the more evident theme for most of the explicit functions of the Society today—the collection of business records, the acquisition of Connecticut imprints, and the preservation of the products of Connecticut craftsmen—have been a marked feature of the Society from its inception.

The purposes of the Society are not understood as clearly as they might be. It is sometimes thought, mistakenly, that only colonial records are collected and that only the pre-revolutionary past is appreciated. The Society's location in Hartford has led to the erroneous conclusion that the primary field of interest is Hartford County, but materials from all periods of Connecticut history and from all sections of the State are collected, cataloged and made available for study.

This essay is intended to provide a narrative account of the major developments in the history of the Society. For reasons of time and to encourage general interest, extensive detail has been avoided. In place of an exhaustive institutional treatment, the present brief, illustrated history is offered. The stress has been placed on the men and women who have played a prominent part in the story and particularly on the ideas which they brought to bear on the issues confronting this institution. Inevitably, selection has led to the omission of what another writer would chose to include. The illustrations which accompany the text are taken entirely from the Society's collections.

Origins, 1825–1839

WE KNOW SURPRISINGLY LITTLE about the steps leading to the formation of The Connecticut Historical Society. Thus far no correspondence or memoranda relating to the organization prior to its actual incorporation have materialized. Even the conscientious Thomas Robbins, the first Librarian of the Society and the man generally identified as its founder, records nothing in his diary about the first organizational efforts until May 30, 1825, the day of the first meeting. It is impossible, therefore, to identify with certainty those who were most active in preparing the proposal for an historical society in Connecticut.

While plans probably were laid at informal meetings by the men who were to become charter members, it is only when we turn to the events of May, 1825 and examine the process of incorporation that we find ourselves on firm ground. At the beginning of that month, the General Assembly, meeting at the State House in Hartford, took up for consideration a petition signed by the Honorable John Trumbull and 30 other Connecticut citizens—14 of whom were from Hartford and 17 from various other towns in the State. The petition took note of the creation of societies in other states for the preservation of historical materials and "prayed" for the incorporation of a similar institution in Connecticut. With the support of such prominent men as Timothy Pitkin (1766–1847), Thomas Day (1777–1855) and William Ellsworth (1791–1869), the outcome could scarely have been in doubt. On the first Wednesday of May, the General Assembly passed into law the resolution creating The Connecticut Historical Society.

The Act of Incorporation touched briefly on the legal position of the new society, named the offices to be filled by annual elections, and specifically charged it with the collection of "whatever may relate to the civil, ecclesiastical and natural history of the United States, and especially of the State of Connecticut." The Bill also stated that the first meeting of the newly-formed Society was to be held at the State House at a time designated by John Trumbull and duly advertised "in one or more newspapers printed in Hartford." The following announcement, naming May 30 as the date for the first meeting, soon appeared in the weekly *Connecticut Courant:*

> It is understood the Society is to be organized at this meeting and all persons friendly to the proposed institution are invited to attend. It is expected some gentlemen will address the meeting.

But, almost in anticipation of future difficulties, the notice was submitted to the *Courant* too late and consequently did not appear until one day after the meeting actually took place. Despite the lack of publicity, the meeting was held as scheduled. All those who attended were drawn from the original group of 31 petitioners. Essential business was settled: officers were elected; a committee was formed to prepare a constitution; and Thomas Robbins offered a few unrecorded remarks "on the objects of the Society." The first elected officers were: President, Hon. John Trumbull; Vice-President, Rt. Rev. Thomas C. Brownell; Recording Secretary, Thomas Day; Corresponding Secretary, Rev. Thomas Robbins; and, Treasurer, Walter Mitchell. At 7 P.M. the meeting was adjourned until the following day.

Timothy Pitkin, Thomas Robbins, Dr. George Sumner, Professor George W. Doane and Thomas Day comprised the committee charged with the preparation of "a Constitution and a Code of By-Laws for the regulation of the Society." The committee met the next day to prepare a draft for presentation at an evening meeting. Thomas Robbins notes in his diary that he "assisted in forming a constitution for the Historical Society and then attended a meeting in the evening." Sixteen members were present on the night of the 31st to sign the document and to elect a Standing Committee. The meeting was then adjourned to Thursday, June 2nd.

The Constitution declared, in Article I, that "It shall be the

JOHN TRUMBULL ESQ.

John Trumbull (1750–1831), poet, judge and first President of the Society, from an engraving by Elkanah Tisdale

duty of every member of this Society to obtain and communicate information relative to the civil, ecclesiastical & natural history of this State & of the United States." The admission fee was set at three dollars and annual dues at two. Meetings of the Society were to be held quarterly "on the Thursday immediately succeeding the first Wednesday in May, August, November, and February: and at the meeting in May shall proceed to elect by ballot" the officers for the following year. New members were to be elected from lists submitted at previous meetings, and no limit was placed on the total number of members who were to be admitted to the Society.

The third meeting within four days took place on June 2nd when 28 Connecticut residents were nominated for membership, and the question of appropriate publicity for the Society was raised. The Standing Committee was urged to take all necessary steps to arouse interest in the Society's activities, beginning with the publication of a pamphlet that would include, along

Thomas Day (1777–1855), Secretary of The State, 1810–1835, first Corresponding Secretary and President of the Society, 1839–1855, painted by O. Dickinson

with the Charter and Constitution, "an appeal to the public." The first quarterly meeting of the Society was held on August 4, when 14 new members were elected.

What brought the 31 original petitioners together in the first place? The same concerns that prompted the creation of historical societies in other states—a sense of anxiety about the preservation of documents, an attitude of state pride, a feeling of respect for the early settlers of New England—motivated the founders of The Connecticut Historical Society. Yet the evidence, slender as it may be on the problem of organization, clearly indicates that it was Thomas Robbins who gave intellectual shape to those concerns by speaking out forcefully in favor of an historical society in Hartford. If there was an historical society movement in New England, then Thomas Robbins was its Connecticut spokesman.

Soon after graduation from Williams College in 1796,

Thomas Robbins found himself drawn both towards the church and antiquarian studies, causing his mother to write to her son in 1802 expressing her fear that "your great curiosity after antiquities may lead you aside from your all important business." The man who was eventually named "that indefatigable antiquarian" never confessed to any such doubts, believing with utter certainty that the events of history revealed the will of God and thus could usefully be studied by the good Christian. Called to a pastorate in East Windsor in 1809, Robbins commenced in the same year assembling a clergyman's library that in time was to number close to 4,000 volumes and an equal number of pamphlets. His growing reputation as a genealogist and historian, secured through sermons, biographical sketches, and particularly his *Historical View of the First Planters of New England,* was signaled by his election in 1815 to the American Antiquarian Society. If through no other source, it was the addresses delivered before that society, published in pamphlet form and distributed to members, which impressed upon the Reverend Dr. Robbins the need to actively promote an historical society in Connecticut. Isaac Goodwin, for example, addressed the members of the American Antiquarian Society in 1820, lamenting the indifference of Americans to their illustrious past. "Generation has followed generation," he declared, "and scarce any efforts have been made to rescue from oblivion, the comparatively recent antiquities of America.—The memorials of our fathers, the origin of our institutions, are scarcely remembered."

Thomas Robbins soon found an opportunity to present similar views to a large and influential audience in Hartford. The occasion was the celebration in Hartford of the Fourth of July —a day, according to one observer, of "uncommon splendor." Robbins, chaplain of the First Regiment of the Connecticut Militia, was the orator of the day. It was an ideal opportunity to arouse an audience of prominent citizens to action. After speaking of the benefits of public festivals and the importance of patriotism, Robbins turned to the need for an institution that would preserve the materials of the past. It is a statement worth quoting at length because it served, in effect, as the manifesto of The Connecticut Historical Society:

I would suggest that we have nothing in this state of the nature of an Historical Society. We have no deposit of ancient books, pamphlets, manuscripts, historical tracts, and temporary publications, many of which are highly valuable, and must become important documents in history. Many of these yet exist, but they are rapidly perishing, and will perish unavoidably, unless some such institution is established for their preservation. But little can be done, in making such collections by individuals, and there are but few persons who have the inclination and leisure to engage in the work. It is a work of labour and perseverance, rather than of much expense. There is no complete set of Election Sermons of the state that have been printed. Nor of the funeral sermons of the respective Governors, which must be among the best documents for their characters. I know of two manuscript accounts, very valuable so far as they extend, of the expedition to Louisburgh; the most gallant military enterprize in the New-England history. Many similarities might probably be found. But they are now very liable to be lost. I presume there are no complete files of the early Newspapers. There are not many of the ancient families whose genealogy is known.—The neighboring states have Institutions of this kind, and have found them highly beneficial.

Robbins concluded this section of his discourse by recommending Hartford, "the oldest town in the state," as the site for the institution.

It was an effective statement because Thomas Robbins was deeply concerned about the cause and could generalize on the basis of direct experience that stretched back into the eighteenth century. As an active collector in his own right, he was in an excellent position to pass harsh judgment on the effectiveness of individual action. As a member of the American Antiquarian Society, he was also thoroughly familiar with the unfortunate catastrophes that overcame many book collections such as the plundering of the Thomas Prince library by British troops in Boston during the Revolution. He was aware, as well, that at least one manuscript collection, that of Jonathan Trumbull, Sr., had been removed from the State because there was no institution in Connecticut devoted to the preservation of historical materials. His speech in 1822 not only described the importance of immediate action, it also anticipated, in its outline of documents to be saved, the pattern of collecting and preservation that was to be followed in the years after 1825.

The recommendation that Hartford be the site for the new institution proved both timely and practical. Hartford in the 1820s was just beginning to reap the benefits of an economic revolution that was to see her transformed from a quiet, commercial center "dealing in lumber and smelling of molasses and old Jamaica" into the sophisticated business capital of an industrializing state. As manufacturing came to supplement trade and commerce, Hartford's entrepreneurs also pioneered in the development of Connecticut banking and insurance, establishing a network of financial institutions that generated investment capital out of passive savings. The city was also on its way to becoming, for the next few decades, the textbook publishing center of the republic with over thirty printing firms active in the 1820s and 1830s. The enterprising spirit of nineteenth century Hartford has left its impression on the Society even today. Recording the progress of Connecticut printing, collecting the products of "inventive genius," and preserving the account books of countless small businesses have long been among the distinctive contributions of The Connecticut Historical Society.

Much of the success of Hartford business was the product of astute combination rather than rugged individualism, and the spirit of association that created the joint-stock companies of Connecticut soon carried over into other fields of activity. The wealth generated by business acumen was put to other uses, and Hartford, once regarded as without cultural distinction, soon became known, according to Samuel G. Goodrich, "for its interesting institutions—literary, charitable and philanthropic." The years following the War of 1812 were marked by the establishment of a succession of philanthropic institutions: the Asylum for the Deaf and Dumb in 1817; the Charitable Society in 1822; the Society for the Relief of the Insane in 1822; and, Washington College in 1823. These and other organizations were founded for distinct purposes, but they reflect a common desire to "improve" society and to put hard dollars to a useful social end. Merchants, bank officers, doctors and clergymen pooled their resources and skills to promote one worthy cause after another, demonstrating a lesson later stated by Henry Barnard that,

> to accomplish any great object, the co-operation of numbers is necessary. This is emphatically true in our republican community. Individual wealth is inadequate to the task.

Hartford also was beginning in the same period to re-establish its importance as a literary and cultural center of Connecticut, regaining the prestige that it lost after the days of the "Hartford wits." The founding of Washington College and the establishment of various seminaries of education provided Hartford with a magnet to draw both students and faculty from other parts of the state and country. Half of the entire faculty of Washington College in 1825, Thomas Church Brownell, George Doane and Nathaniel Wheaton, were charter members of the Historical Society and comprised three of the six members of the Standing Committee. The presence in Hartford of such literary luminaries as John Trumbull, John G. C. Brainard, Samuel G. Goodrich and Lydia H. Sigourney did much to enhance the cultural self-esteem of the city. Nor did the literary community constitute a distinct element within Hartford society. As with the supporters of the various charitable institutions, professional men, business leaders, and independent gentlemen moved together in one circle. The innumerable literary clubs and societies that became a marked feature of Hartford life from the 1820s brought together, on an equal basis, authors, bankers, doctors, and college instructors, forming what Charles Sigourney, in a toast at John Trumbull's farewell dinner in 1825, called "the natural aristocracy of intellect and virtue."

Although the arguments for an historical society in Connecticut had been effectively marshalled by 1822, and the climate of opinion was becoming increasingly receptive to the idea, it was still almost three years before incorporation. There was, in the meantime, another popular event which may well have kindled

Hartford's enthusiasm for the past and given greater momentum to the program laid down by Thomas Robbins. In August of 1824, the Marquis de Lafayette returned to the United States to begin an official tour that proved a complete personal triumph. Disembarking in New York (where he was received by the officers of the New-York Historical Society and made an honorary member) Lafayette proceeded up the New England coast to Boston, later returning to New York by way of Hartford. Elaborate preparations were made for his visit, and emotions in Hartford steadily increased as the weekly reports of Lafayette's journey in the *Connecticut Courant* carried the news of his triumphant reception throughout New England. Arriving in Hartford on the morning of September 5, Lafayette alighted from his stage at Bennet's Hotel, passed under a ceremonial arch adorned with evergreens to the sound of enthusiastic huzzas, and was then addressed by the Mayor, Jonathan Brace, who declared:

> This occasion, Sir, is peculiarly calculated to recall to mind, those great and interesting events, which have taken place since your first efforts in favor of an infant country, with feeble means contending against superior and lawless powers.

After visiting the State House, Lafayette returned to Main Street to review the assembled units of Connecticut militia. In the middle of the parade, a singularly affecting moment occurred which demonstrated the accuracy of the Mayor's remarks.

> A company of old revolutionary officers and soldiers consisting of about 80, and commanded by Judge Hillyer, passed in review near the platform, and each of them shook hands with the General. . . . There was a rush from every quarter to witness the scene—many of them had been wounded—some with one eye—and the health of all more or less impaired in the service of their country.

Few within the crowd remained unmoved by the encounter.

Three charter members of the Historical Society, Thomas

STATE HOUSE, HARTFORD, CONNECTICUT. 1834.

The Old State House, Hartford, in a water color view, as it might
have appeared to Lafayette in 1824, painted by E. W. Clay in 1834

Day, John Trumbull, and Nathan Johnson, each played an important part in the visit of Lafayette to Hartford. How many
others were present is impossible to say, but the emotions released by the general's appearance in Hartford could not have
failed to excite interest in an historical society. The visit served
as a visible reminder of Connecticut's revolutionary past; the
triumphal tour, explained Frederick Butler, a Wethersfield historian in 1825, "brings our revolution near to us." The enthusiasm for Lafayette demonstrated the power of the hero to draw
a crowd and inspire a sense of unity among the participants, and
the original members of The Connecticut Historical Society,
who were to express concern about the loss of respect for tradition, may have sensed, in the response to Lafayette, a way of
employing history to promote a renewed consensus. The visit,
continued Butler in his account of the tour,

> has brought those together that have been separated by
> long lives of political animosity. It helps to break down
> the great land-marks of party and makes a holiday of
> kind and generous feelings in the hearts of multitudes

that throng his way, as he moves in triumphal procession from city to city.

The poignant meeting of the old general and the aged veterans of the Revolution provoked another response—nostalgia for what was viewed as the more tranquil past coupled with a sense of impending loss. It was painfully obvious that, with the passing away of those last veterans, a living link with the Revolution would be severed. A strikingly similar concern was expressed in the first publication of The Connecticut Historical Society, *An Address to the Public,* in which it was stated, "when a few more grey-headed men shall have passed away from us, we shall only have in addition to the meager records which we now possess, the uncertain echo of remote tradition." The only recourse, suggested the essay, was to admonish "the fathers of the land to recall and record for the benefit of their children, the scenes in which they partook." In that way the inscribed recollections of our heroes, rather than their uncertain echoes, would be preserved for generations to come.

Thomas Robbins's speech in 1822, Lafayette's visit in 1824, and the expansive atmosphere of Hartford in the 1820s all played their part in stimulating the formation of an historical society in Connecticut. Ultimately our analysis of the origins of the Society must center in the men who were present at its inception. The purposes that the Society was intended to serve were rooted in the character and outlook of the original petitioners. The charter members were, as one might expect, men of considerable importance in early nineteenth century Connecticut. Well-educated, acknowledged leaders in their towns, they were representative of that social and political elite often referred to as Connecticut's "Standing Order." They included governors and senators, judges and prominent lawyers. All the important professions of the day were represented within the group of original members. There were seven doctors and six clergymen, as well as several merchants and teachers. Over half were trained in law, and most of these at Tapping Reeve's Law School at Litchfield. Over two-thirds were Yale graduates and had passed through a similar course of humanistic studies which stressed classical languages, logic and theology. Their knowledge and feeling for history was less the consequence of formal academic study than the result of reading the Latin and Greek historians, absorbing the lessons of the Bible, and acquiring, from childhood, an easy familiarity with their own family origins, with local tales and anecdotes, and with the names and events of their New England past. History, for these men, was not a dry, scientific discipline, but an integral part of their lives, a branch of moral philosophy. To them, history was philosophy teaching by example and the source, therefore, of practical advice for the conduct of daily affairs.

There was a particular bond which rallied these men behind the Historical Society; with only a few exceptions the first members of the Society (lawyers and clergymen alike) were Federalists, and their assumptions about the role an historical society should play were derived, in large measure, from their political philosophy. The dominance of the Federalist party in Connecticut prior to 1818, its strong base in Yale College, and its solid support from the Calvinist clergy, the legal profession, and even from among Connecticut's schoolmasters are themes too well known to need elaboration. Their views on politics were drawn from an image of society which was hierarchical and paternalistic. Connecticut Federalism, according to Chester McArthur Destler, "while liberal in spirit and constitutional in character, was pre-democratic, transitional between the decadent society in Europe and the democracy of a later America." Attached to stability, order and piety, and convinced of the wisdom of rule by the "Standing Order," Federalists distrusted the lower orders, questioned the need for an opposition political party, and generally decried the principles of equality and reason.

In what way was the organization of The Connecticut Historical Society connected to the Federalist persuasion? Connecticut Federalists viewed the challenges they faced—the rise of Jeffersonian democracy, the demand for a separation of church and state, and the rise of party politics—in moral terms; they attributed the successes of their upstart rivals to the weakness of the general citizenry and to the loss of old habits of reverence and subordination. As Federalism increasingly became a sectional party confined to New York and New England, it became obvious to men like Thomas Robbins that its revival in Connecticut rested on reawakening the populace to the virtues which had once characterized "the land of steady habits." An historical society in Connecticut, through its various activities, might well be able to counteract the forces of radicalism. The collection of such historical materials as old sermons, ancient relics, and manuscripts could serve, at least in part, to remind people of their heroic past, to foster a respect for tradition, and to inspire a veneration for departed ancestors. Periodic historical celebrations (like that during Lafayette's tour), possibly organized by the Historical Society, might serve to break down party divisions and re-unite the people around a common, Federalist creed. Occasional historical publications could diffuse among the reading public a heightened sense of historical awareness.

The writings of Thomas Robbins bear witness to the connection between political conservatism and historical consciousness, but the best illustration of the Federalist concerns of The Connecticut Historical Society can be found in the pamphlet issued by the Society in 1825, *Address to the Public,* to announce its formation and articulate its goals. Beyond the goal of collecting the materials of Connecticut history, as the pamphlet makes clear, lay certain ultimate moral objectives—the revival of patriotism and ancestor-worship among the citizenry. Much of the history of the colony had been lost, explained the author, but,

> if any portion can be raked from the ruins of the past, to illustrate our history; if any names of ancient valour, of ancient piety, can be gathered from among the graves of our fathers to animate the patriotism and virtue of their sons, we shall not have laboured in vain.

The final goal of the Historical Society in 1825 was not to promote dispassionate research; the lessons of the past were clearly in mind before the collecting began and the histories were written.

The historical societies founded in New England before 1825 tended to be rather exclusive organizations and, with a membership drawn from the State's "natural aristocracy," there was every likelihood that The Connecticut Historical Society would ignore the general public. The political concerns of the

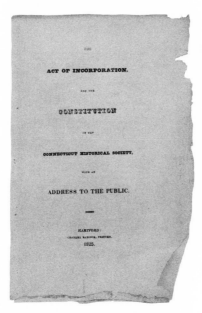

Title page of the first publication of the Society

Federalist members, together with the need to encourage gifts and deposits of historical materials, insured that the Society would take steps to cultivate the public. "Whatever advantages may ensue," explained the *Address to the Public,* "will, under suitable regulations, be open to all." Cautious and ambiguous as that may sound today, it was a bold statement for the time. It is important to remember that the membership of the Society, though elected, was not and has never been, strictly confined to a fixed number. The "natural aristocracy," then, was to be open to all who earned a place.

The *Address* concluded by outlining a broad and ambitious program of collecting, calling upon interested citizens (in words that suggest Thomas Robbins was the author) for donations of early newspapers, sermons, memoirs, and, significantly, books and pamphlets published within the State. Yet despite the promising beginning, the Society met only five times in 1825 before all official activity ceased and a period of dormancy commenced. The Society, therefore, did not truly begin to perform its function of collecting and preserving the sources of Connecticut history until its revival in 1839. The accomplishments of 1825 may appear slight, but the fact of incorporation and the articulation of a program of action were important accomplishments. In 1839 the Society could begin again with an already defined purpose and structure.

Why did the Society lapse into inactivity? The most immediate explanation was the departure of its President, Judge John Trumbull, to Detroit to join his married daughter. On September 24, 1825, he submitted his resignation to Thomas Day while wishing success to the institution and honor and prosperity for its members. Two subsequent announcements appeared in the *Connecticut Courant* in 1826, the second reminding members that,

> by the Constitution of the Society, the presence of 15 members is necessary to constitute a quorum for the election of officers, and of seven members for the transaction of ordinary business.

There is no evidence that any members gathered at the appointed times. The duties of the President should have devolved upon Bishop Brownell, Vice-President of the Society as well as President of Washington College, but possibly he was too preoccupied with college business to take a more active role. Significantly, in 1839, one of the two changes introduced in the constitution was an amendment providing that if any officer be incapacitated, or resign or leave the State, the Standing Committee would be empowered to fill the vacancy. There is one other curious explanation for the suspension of activity in 1825 which is supplied by Thomas Robbins in a letter to Edward Herrick of New Haven in 1839. "The Historical Society," wrote Robbins, "was originally instituted prematurely, a measure of Bishop Brownell and Sigourney, to favour their college. I was not in favour of the proceeding, but joined with them in hopes of doing something." No evidence has surfaced to confirm the accusation, however, and the likeliest explanation for the remark was a latent Calvinist suspicion of that Episcopal college on the hill, as well as Robbins's sense of disappointment that he could not be present in Hartford to take a more active role in the Society's affairs after its revival in 1839.

Revival
1839–1855

IN THE SPRING OF 1839, after a lapse of nearly 14 years, The Connecticut Historical Society was revived. A new charter was secured from the General Assembly, and meetings and other activities were resumed. Among the letters of congratulation was one from a Thomas Webb who "rejoiced to find it [the Society] was not dead, but only slept; and having at length aroused from its slumbers, I trust it will speed onwards with renewed vigor and redoubled energy." It proved to be an accurate prediction, for the next 15 years in the life of the Society were indeed marked by energetic collecting, useful writing and popular lectures.

The expression "not dead, but only slept" was particularly apt. During the interval between 1825 and 1839 the idea of an historical society was kept alive through the activities of several Hartford residents who formed what they called an "historical club." It was an informal association of former members and friends of the then inactive Connecticut Historical Society. Lacking a set or rules and regulations, without officers or written minutes, almost no record of this club has survived and no mention of the organization has yet appeared in print. It is only due to Henry Barnard's various efforts to compose an autobiography that any reference to the club has been preserved. Unfortunately, the historical record suffers from a double burden, for the autobiography was never completed and what was written has been widely dispersed (some pages have evidently been lost, others were saved, but distributed to different institutions).

The pages that have survived indicate that the club was active during the years from 1832 to 1839 and that it met over the store of Humphrey & Seyms on Main Street in Hartford. Barnard's notes, compiled at the end of his life, do not indicate the complete list of members, but Thomas Day, Charles and James Hosmer, Timothy Pitkin, and Colonel James Ward, along with Barnard himself were apparently active in the club. The evenings set aside by the group were devoted to local and historical topics, with one session given over to a reading of a manuscript diary by Timothy Pitkin while he was in Washington, D.C. (but which has since disappeared). According to Henry Barnard, the idea for the celebration of the 200th anniversary of the settlement of Hartford was first broached at one of the club's meetings; he further claims that its meetings "finally culminated in the revival and rechartering of the old Connecticut Historical Society."

The 200th anniversary of the founding of Hartford would have been an appropriate moment to revive the Society, but Hartford's second Centennial, celebrated on November 9, 1835, came and went without stimulating the members of the still-languishing Historical Society. The preparations for the event were largely in the hands of Connecticut democrats, and the orator of the day, the Reverend Joel Hawes, despite a perfectly appropriate address, was later criticized by Henry Barnard for his lack of an "historical sense." It was probably Hawes's political affiliation, not his speech, which was at fault. Meanwhile, in New Haven, a similar occasion was marked by a public festival held on April 25, 1838 organized by several committees, including one from the Connecticut Academy of Arts and Sciences founded in 1799 for the "collection and propagation of useful knowledge."

There was still no activity in Hartford when, on March 6, 1839, Edward C. Herrick, a member of the Yale faculty and later its librarian, wrote to Barnard inquiring whether "The Connecticut Historical Society (established at Hartford in 1825) has ever held any meetings subsequent to that date,—or made any election of officers since then,—or made any collection of historical documents or books." Herrick, who may have been fishing in the hopes of expanding Yale's collections, was soon to be found among the petitioners to the General Assembly for a renewal of the Society's charter. Presumably, he would have known of any plans to resurrect the Society within several weeks of any decision. It is possible that Herrick's letter stimulated Barnard to take action, for it appears that the decision to renew the charter was reached in March or April, 1839.

Fearing that the original charter might have expired due to non-use, a new petition with 33 signatures affixed to it (15 former members and 18 new supporters) was submitted to the May, 1839 session of the General Assembly. The petition noted that some "valuable historical materials" had been collected by the Society, but were now in "danger of being scattered and lost, without the care of this, or some similar institution." On May 1, 1839, the Assembly affirmed the continued legal existence of The Connecticut Historical Society, declaring "the powers and privileges originally granted thereto, be continued and perpetuated, as though its officers had been chosen annually since 1825."

Eventually, Henry Barnard was to claim much of the credit for the Society's renewal. In 1889, while in his late 70s, he was called upon to prepare a paper on the early history of the institution. The notes which he left assert his personal responsibility for the initial successes of the revived Society. "The earliest movement in the direction of a state historical society," he wrote, "was in 1837–8 in conference with Mr. Day, Charles Hosmer and James Hosmer." On another page he claims that it was he who made the first suggestion and conducted all the "incipient correspondence concerning the matter." We can be more secure in stating, however, that Henry Barnard's active role insured that a distinctly progressive viewpoint would be brought to bear on the issues confronting the newly activated organization. Corresponding Secretary from 1839 to 1846, President from 1854 to 1860, and Vice-President from 1863 to 1874, it seems remarkable that Barnard, the man labeled the "Nestor of American education," could spare time from his varied commitments to take a leading part in the affairs of the Historical Society over such a long period of time.

Born in Hartford of a substantial family, Henry Barnard was educated in a district school, at Monson Academy, Hopkins

Henry Barnard (1811–1900), prominent educator, member of the Society from 1839 to 1900 and President, 1854–1860, painted by F. Tuttle in 1886

Grammar School and at Yale. While in college, he excelled in scholarship and public speaking and served for two years as Librarian of Linonia. Already a rather serious youth, Barnard was deeply impressed with an address by Henry Brougham, then Lord Rector of Glasgow University. Barnard was later to claim that these words of Brougham's formed the inspiration of his own career:

> To diffuse useful information; to further intellectual refinement, sure forerunner of moral improvement; to hasten the coming of the bright day when the dawn of general knowledge shall chase away the lazy, lingering mists, even from the base of the great social pyramid— this indeed is a high calling, in which the most splendid talents and consummate virtue may well press onward eager to bear a part.

After graduation, Barnard studied law and passed the bar, travelled extensively in Europe, and returned to Hartford in 1836 to commence a public career. In 1837 he was elected to the General Assembly from Hartford where he promoted such philanthropic causes as the incorporation of libraries, the care of the insane, and the improvement of the State's common schools. A pronounced Whig in politics and completely at home among the country's social elite, Henry Barnard was also an idealist and believed that merit, rather than birth, should be the determinant of position and reputation.

Throughout his life, Barnard viewed The Connecticut Historical Society as an educational instrument which could raise the general level of culture and knowledge in the State. Actively laboring to make the Society truly state-wide, he encouraged the recruitment of active members from each county; he favored the publication of a popular magazine of history and genealogy; and he argued for the enlistment of a group of effective speakers on historical subjects who could represent the Society and address local groups throughout Connecticut. His model of what an historical society should be was much closer to the State financed institutions of the mid-west than to the privately supported organizations developing in New England. It is clear, moreover, that Barnard's views on the role of The Connecticut Historical Society were not entirely shared by the membership. His gifts were welcomed by others members, and he was voted into office repeatedly; yet his advice on the aims of the Society was politely rejected or quietly tabled. The bulk of the members during the nineteenth century preferred the Society remain a private association of gentlemen who shared historical interests. The public was not to be ignored and, like Barnard, members agreed that merit ought to be rewarded; but, as one committee reported in 1858, "Election which does not imply selection, . . . has little meaning." Barnard had more success in applying his ideas in the appropriate area of public education.

The first meeting of the Society, following the renewal of the charter, was held on June 1, 1839 in the rooms of the Young Men's Institute at Gilman's Hall at which time Thomas Day was elected President and Charles Hosmer was selected Recording Secretary. During the next several months, the business of the Society was sufficiently taxing to require meetings nearly every week. Since the original constitution had never been properly ratified, it was apparent that the first assignment was the formulation of a new set of by-laws, a task entrusted to Thomas Day and Henry Barnard. Not until the fifth meeting, on June 15, was agreement reached: the new by-laws increased the number of vice-presidents to seven (making possible wider geographic representation), enlarged the standing committee and clearly defined its responsibilities, and articulated the first of what were to be many statements on the subject of deposits. At the next two meetings, additional officers were elected: Henry Barnard, Corresponding Secretary; James B. Hosmer, Treasurer; Professor James L. Kingsley and David D. Field, Vice-Presidents. On July 26, Thomas Day was called upon to draw up a "circular letter for publication" similar in form to the 1825 *Address to the Public.*

Judge Day's views were presented to members on September 20, prior to their publication and distribution. His remarks were brief but to the point, as though he feared the Society might fail again if it did not clearly understand and undertake its responsibilities. The object of the Society, simply stated, was the history of the State and country, and the function of the organization, therefore, was "the discovery, the collection and the preservation of the materials of such history." Thomas Day dropped the distinction, maintained in 1825, between civil and ecclesiastical history. The advantages present in Connecticut were clear, he argued: because of habits of literacy dating from the first settlement of the colonies, the materials of history are "expressed with great precision; are written in legible characters; and come to us in a good state of preservation." Nevertheless, he insisted, they had been scattered, and in many cases their importance was not adequately appreciated. He proceeded to enumerate the types of sources desired, explaining that the "Society relies not only upon the exertions of its members, but confidently appeals to our citizens generally for their encouragement and assistance." He asked that all articles intended for the Library or "Cabinet" be sent to Charles Hosmer, Recording Secretary and Clerk of the Standing Committee. They would be safe, he assured his readers, "from the corrosions of time and

The first home of the Society, 1839–1843. Photographed at the end of the nineteenth-century, the building, to the left of Center Church, had suffered somewhat from neglect in the intervening years

the power of accident," because the Society had recently secured "a convenient room in the City of Hartford, central and of easy access, with suitable cases, shelves and other accomodations."

The new home and first settled location for The Connecticut Historical Society were modest quarters over the store of Humphrey and Seyms, the same rooms used by the informal historical club that met in the 1830s. Situated at 124 Main Street, in the first building south of Center Church, it was, as Day had indicated, "central and of easy access." The owner of the building was Cyprian Nichols, and the rent was fixed at $40 a year (to be increased to $50 in 1840). The first meeting at the new location occurred on September 13, 1839 when Charles Hosmer was asked "to provide suitable furniture for the room of the Society." Chairs costing seven dollars were purchased from Robbins and Winship, cabinetmakers with a shop at 94 Main Street. The first glass case was acquired and shelves were erected

First report of the Treasurer submitted by James Hosmer (1781–1878) in 1840

so that the books, pamphlets and objects gathered with energy could now be displayed. Evidently, no regular hours were kept for public viewing of the growing collection, but arrangements for an inspection of the relics could be made with Charles Hosmer. James Hammond Trumbull visited the room in 1841 when he was just 20 and discussed the possessions of the Society with Mr. Hosmer whom he described as "librarian and curator."

With regular meetings, a fixed location, and with dues accumulating, the revived organization had achieved, by the Fall of 1839, a respectable position. Further progress depended upon increasing public awareness of its existence and purposes. President Day's remarks were printed and 500 copies were distributed. News of the Society's reorganization was carried by Henry Barnard who addressed the State Lyceum on November 13 and secured the passage of a resolution urging local antiquarians to forward the results of their studies to Hartford. Attention was also drawn to the Society by means of a four-page circular distributed to local clergymen with the aim of collecting historical and statistical data on the towns of Connecticut. Similar in form to the printed queries distributed by the Connecticut Academy of Arts and Sciences in 1800, it met with less success.

At this time plans were also launched to commemorate the 200th anniversary of the adoption of Connecticut's first civil constitution. The rationale for the celebration was discussed by Henry Barnard at the public banquet which was a part of the affair:

> The Connecticut Historical Society, on its recent reorganization, felt called upon to make some demonstration of its intention and ability to excite a deeper and wider interest in historical investigation, and to gather up the memorials of the past history of the State. As the centennial anniversaries of the first settlement of the principal towns of the State had gone by, the Society, in looking around for some event which on its annual return should bring along with it a freshened remembrance of the honourable names and events which cluster along the pages of Connecticut History, felt that none could be more appropriate than the first organization of civil government by the intelligent freeman of Windsor, Wethersfield and Hartford, in 1639.

On October 4, 1839, President Day was asked to write to Noah Webster in New Haven, then in his 81st year, requesting him "to deliver a discourse on behalf of the Society" for the occasion. The choice was an astute one, for Webster was recommended by ancestry, personal achievement, and by his political associations. The venerable scholar agreed to speak, conditional on the state of his health. Since caution dictated providing a substitute in case of illness, Day asked Leonard Bacon, also of New Haven, to be prepared to step in, explaining "we deem it very important that some public interest should be excited in favor of this institution."

According to the dictates of the calendar, the celebration should have taken place in January, but the hazards of travelling

One of the portraits in the possession of the Society in 1840 and exhibited at Gilman's Hall on April 21, 1840, Reverend Elnathan Whitman (1708/9–1777) in a painting attributed to William Johnston

in Winter prompted Webster to ask for a postponement. He was prepared to see Bacon deliver the address, but the Society was anxious to have Webster and the ceremony was delayed until April 21. The entire celebration, extended over two days, combined light-hearted entertainment with solemn moralizing. On Monday evening, April 20, President Day played host to members and their guests at a period-costume ball, at which ladies with "frizzed and powdered hair, stiff-starched ruffs and embroidered skirts" were escorted by gentlemen with high stockings, buckled shoes and lace shirts. On the following day, members of the Society and their guests gathered at the Senate Chamber in the State House and moved in procession to the Center Church, where the officers took to the platform along with representatives from other historical societies. Here, after a hymn, prayers and a reading of the Constitution, Noah Webster offered his remarks. At 2 P.M. the company retired to a public

Paired with the portrait of Reverend Elnathan Whitman at the exhibition was this painting of his wife, Abigail Stanley Whitman (1719–1795), attributed to Joseph Steward.

banquet at Gilman's Hall, where the walls had been thoughtfully lined with portraits of some of the historic figures in the State, many from the Historical Society's own collection.

By April of 1840, Noah Webster had become a rather crusty New England conservative, and he took the opportunity provided by the Historical Society to preach to his audience on the dangers of innovation and the value of tradition. In true Federalist fashion, he passed without hesitation from religion to politics and back again. Consumed by pessimism, he offered little hope for the republic unless the Bible replaced reason and philosophy as the guide to life. An inexorable decline would occur, he predicted, unless the rage for political faction was abandoned, the delusion that men are equal rejected, and the indifference to the Sabbath mended. A proper respect for the past and a "due reverence for the principles of our ancestors" would inspire, he hoped, a regeneration of old patterns of discipline.

Of course, Noah Webster did not speak for the Society, but it can be assumed that many of his attitudes were shared, at least in a milder form, by its membership. Curiously, some of the letters sent to Henry Barnard by members or supporters of the institution who could not attend the celebration actually paralleled Webster's views. Timothy Pitkin wrote to Barnard on April 13 praying "that the political principles accepted by our ancestors will never be abandoned by their descendants." In declining his invitation to participate in the ceremony, George Doane called the formation of historical societies "an office of filial piety towards the fathers of the republic." It seems likely, then, that some of the political and moral objectives that had played a role in the founding of the Society in 1825 were also present in 1839 and 1840.

In their concern for the preservation of historical documents, the Society's members turned with urgency in those early days to the task of collecting. New members were selected for their antiquarian zeal—Thomas Day, for example, writing to E. Champion Bacon in 1839, asked for his recommendations of "suitable and *useful* men." Upon election new members were sent a copy of Day's address along with an earnest solicitation that they begin "making collections of historical materials," and "forwarding them to the room of the Society" in the care of Charles Hosmer. One of the first amendments to the by-laws introduced a record book of accessions to the operations of the Society, and these volumes, now amounting to 11, comprise the most accurate guide to the pattern and intensity of acquisition. In early 1844 a committee, formed to review the state of the institution, observed that in the period from 1839, 172 resident members had been added to rolls of the Society. Roughly 6,000 pamphlets, 250 bound volumes of newspapers, numerous volumes and manuscripts, coins, medals, portraits, and items of old furniture had been deposited with or donated to the Society. Prospects, noted the committee, were of "a cheerful and flattering kind."

Charles Hosmer's store room and the second floor of the simple wooden building at 124 Main Street were rapidly becoming filled when, in the Summer of 1841, Daniel Wadsworth announced his plan to see a gallery of fine arts erected on the lot lying to the west of his own house. Under the influence of Henry Barnard, the plan was broadened in scope so that a building might also provide space for the Hartford Young Men's Institute and The Connecticut Historical Society. A campaign to raise funds to put up the building was initiated in September, 1841, and Thomas Day, James Hosmer, and James Ward were among the members of the Society who made substantial donations to the building fund. Two New York architects, Ithiel Town (later of New Haven) and Alexander Jackson Davis, designed the now-familiar building and construction began in March of 1842. A corporation, the "Wadsworth Atheneum," was created by State statute in May of the same year, and the Historical Society was eventually able to move into its new rooms at the Atheneum in December of 1843.

The removal of the last books to the substantial and more secure quarters of the Atheneum preceded by several months an-

The Wadsworth Atheneum, home of the Society from December, 1843 to June, 1950, from a lithograph by E. B. and E. C. Kellogg

other significant development: the return of the Reverend Thomas Robbins to Hartford as the Society's first, full-time Librarian. The "indefatigable antiquarian" had left East Windsor in 1827 and, from 1832, had ministered to the spiritual needs of a congregation in Mattapoisett, Massachusetts. Despite several appeals from Henry Barnard for "his wisdom and experience," Robbins was unable to take an active part in the revival of the Society. With the addition of around 100 volumes each year, his personal library continued to grow until it numbered, in 1842, almost 3,500 volumes with an equal number of pamphlets.

The disposition of that library was a matter of intense concern to the bachelor clergyman. An entry in his diary for November 4, 1845 reads: "Last evening endeavored to consecrate myself anew to the disposal of God, particularly with regard to my property." The weighty responsibility of serving God as the trustee of an important collection prompted Robbins to write and rewrite his will, each time altering the ultimate destination of that library. In the first will, composed in 1826, he identified Timothy Pitkin and Thomas Day as trustees and stipulated that they should donate the collection to a "large and permanent library," provided that it "be kept entire and be continued in the state of Connecticut." In 1842 that arrangement was superceded by another will in which Harvard University was to receive "the books numbered in the catalogue," on condition that it be kept intact "and that additions . . . be of the same character, essentially, an Historical and Theological library." All family correspondence was to remain with his relatives, but The Connecticut Historical Society was to receive all the pamphlets, periodicals, newspapers, and "antiquities" in the collection, "believing," as he put it, "that I made the first movements for the establishment of that institution."

In October of 1842, Robbins received a letter from his sister who said she knew of his recent will (but not its details). She mentioned to her brother that the Atheneum was going up in Hartford and would provide ample room for his library, adding that her children believed The Connecticut Historical Society would be the best place for the collection. Thomas Robbins did not respond to her advice until well after his move to Hartford.

The arrangement that brought Robbins to Hartford grew out of mutual interests. The Society needed his assistance to arrange its collections, and Thomas Robbins was in need of a new position. As Henry Barnard later put it, "My offer it seems was the more readily accepted by Dr. Robbins because of petty gossip from which the most exemplary rural pastors if unmarried, whether old or young, do not escape." An innocent kiss had been maliciously distorted, and Dr. Robbins was on the verge of being dismissed from his pastorate by his congregation when Henry Barnard, largely on his own initiative, set in motion the negotiations that brought Robbins to his post at the Atheneum. Barnard was then serving in Rhode Island as Commissioner of Education and sitting on a legislative committee which raised the question of purchasing Dr. Robbins's library as the basis of a State Library. Barnard attested to the value of the collection, but warned that it would not long be available. Loyalty to The Connecticut Historical Society encouraged Barnard to win sufficient support from its members for offering the position of Librarian to the bachelor Robbins. Early in June of 1844, Robbins began preparations to leave Mattapoisett, only receiving on the 28th the letter offering him the position in Hartford. "It is all of the great mercy of God," he confessed in his diary, and he wrote to Charles Hosmer on July 3 agreeing in principle to come to Connecticut. Robbins preferred to be a full-time Librarian and to be reimbursed at a salary which would permit him to continue to purchase books for his collection. The Historical Society, meanwhile, was barely self-supporting, and the Treasurer, James Hosmer, frequently had to cover expenditures made on its behalf out of his own pocket. It was imperative to arrange a subscription to cover Robbins's salary, and Henry Barnard again took the initiative in the matter of collaring members for contributions. When the total sum subscribed still fell short of $300, Barnard wrote to Robbins guaranteeing the salary of $300 against his own name.

On July 25, 1844, Barnard wrote to Robbins enthusiastically, declaring him "the man of the Historical Society" and affirming that with him as Librarian and his books on the shelves, the institution would shortly be the "ornament" of the State. But the question of the legal ownership of the valuable

Thomas Robbins, seated in an ancient turned chair owned by the Society and dressed in the style of the eighteenth century, from a daguerreotype taken in 1846

collection that was to accompany Robbins to Hartford was still unsettled when Barnard submitted a delicately worded announcement to the *Hartford Daily Courant* on September 12. "Whatever may be its final destination," wrote Barnard, "the members of the Connecticut Historical Society, and our citizens, will soon have an opportunity to consult and profit by it." Surrounded by his friends and admirers, happily performing the duties of Librarian and Cabinet-Keeper, it was inevitable that his will would once more be rewritten. On October 8, 1845, Robbins willed his library to The Connecticut Historical Society, provided that it be kept intact and that additions to his collection preserve the orthodox theological tone of the library.

There remained one final act to the drama, however. Apparently, Robbins's salary was paid somewhat irregularly which prompted him to offer the library by deed of gift after death upon receiving guarantees of an annual salary of $600. The contract, dated May 27, 1846, was of value to all, enabling the Society to secure a final committment as to the disposition of the library, and Thomas Robbins to finally receive a salary that permitted him to collect again at his old pace.

With the employment of Thomas Robbins, the Historical Society, at its new location in the Atheneum, commenced keeping regular hours. During Robbins's tenure as Librarian, it was open six days a week, generally from 10 A.M. to noon and from 2 to 6 P.M. Visitors to the city could now look forward to a stop at the "Historical Rooms" where they could expect to be entertained and edified with learned descriptions of the relics and books on display. Long after Robbins had died, the Society received a letter from a man who remembered following the Librarian around the Atheneum as a small child. "There never has been since," the writer said, "and I doubt if there ever will be again, the same care and veneration for a human being, as that which I felt in following him about, among his treasures at the Atheneum, listening to his observations regarding the various sacred things."

Benson Lossing, the irrepressible traveller and author, visited the rooms of the Society in 1847 and left an interesting record of his encounter:

> The cordial welcome with which I was received by Dr. Robbins was a prelude to many kind courtesies bestowed by him during a visit of three hours. He is a venerable bachelor of seventy-two years, and, habited in the style of a gentleman fifty years ago, his appearance carried the mind back to the time of Washington.

Robbins proceeded to guide Lossing through the collections much as he had led others, pointing out the many prized possessions: the chest of Elder Brewster, an ancient turned chair from New Haven, the tavern sign of General Putnam, the blood-stained vest worn by Colonel Ledyard at the battle of Groton. Guide and interpreter of the collections, custodian of the Society's "sacred things," Robbins was much more than a

The tavern sign displayed at the inn kept by General Israel Putnam (1718–1790) in Woodstock

librarian. He had truly become "the man of the historical society."

In numerical terms, the collection of books and relics at the Historical Society in the 1840s was still quite small. During the first years of the Society, however, historians and genealogists had few institutions to which they could turn for sources or for information. The public library movement had not yet gotten started in the State; there was no State Library in Connecticut worthy of the name until the appointment of James Hammond Trumbull as State Librarian in 1854; and the library of Yale College was far more insular than it is today. The collection building up at the Historical Society in the 1840s thus possessed an importance out of proportion to its actual size.

One of the pressing tasks facing the Society, made more imperative by the deposit and eventual gift of Robbins's library, was the arrangement of its books, pamphlets and manuscripts so that they could be used with some convenience. A committee formed in 1844, before the arrival of the new Librarian, recommended that when the rooms at the Atheneum were completely finished "a properly digested catalogue of the Library and Collections be made, the want of which has been the source of much inconvenience and embarrassment." Because of the institution's limited funds, the chairman of the committee, Samuel Parsons, suggested "an immediate appeal to the enlightened and patriotic legislature of the State of Connecticut for a liberal donation to aid this Society in accomplishing the purposes of this establishment." The request was deferred until June of 1845 when a newly formed Library Committee convinced the Standing Committee to submit the request to the General Assembly. Pointing out that the organization was "not designed for, nor appropriated to the use and advantage of the individual members of the Society, they being merely trustees of the public," the Library Committee asked for a grant of $2,500 to carry out its important purposes. The legislature, acting on the recommendation of the Committee on Education, awarded a special grant of $1,000 to be allocated to the care of the manuscripts, confirming that the institution's rooms "are freely thrown open to all, and its exertions are intended for the public good."

Two activities central to the Society are regular lectures and frequent publications, both of which commenced in the 1840s. Aside from Thomas Robbins's remarks on the purposes of the institution, no lectures were offered in 1825. Following President Day's address in September, 1839, meetings were occasionally turned over to a member for the presentation of a lecture on an historical topic. In the Fall of 1843, a determined effort was made to introduce a regular program of lectures and a committee was formed to make the arrangements. A course of lectures for members and invited guests took place that Winter and Spring at Center Church and included addresses by David D. Field, Horace Bushnell and Thomas Day. Part of the motive behind this effort was undoubtedly financial, for funds were needed to equip the new rooms of the Society at the Atheneum. Attendance was good, the experiment proved reasonably successful, and regular lectures became a customary part of the Society's activities.

Initially, the lecture program served a decidedly social as well as educational function. Although it had become acceptable to admit escorted ladies to these lectures, a formal resolution was passed in 1849 permitting them to be present at the reading of the papers. A notice in the *Courant* shortly thereafter added that "it is rare that the Society thus opens its sessions to the public, and we sincerely trust that when it has papers of historical interest to be read, the practice will continue." In the 1850s lectures were followed by "entertainments" of some sort with the proceeds from the sale of tickets devoted to the cost of refreshments. In January, 1855, at one soirée, judging from the submitted bill, members and guests consumed 10 quarts of ice cream, seven gallons of coffee, three quarts of jelly and 300 macaroons, a rather impressive achievement. Critics felt, however, that these lectures should be exclusively educational events and should be opened completely to the public. "Fortunate would it be," wrote one who called himself "Excelsior" in the *Courant,* "if some of the 'exquisite' and fine drawn lectures which abound among us, were supplanted by popular lectures concerning the thrillingly interesting history of our own State." A persistent tension between the preferences of the membership and the public responsibilities of the institution, never adequately defined, had long been and was to remain an unresolved issue.

The publication of original documents, lectures and historical treatises was one of the primary aims enunciated in 1839 by President Day. Preservation through the multiplication of printed copies and the diffusion of historical knowledge had been one of the goals announced by the Massachusetts Historical Society in 1791. In 1840 a committee of The Connecticut Historical Society was formed to consider the expediency of publishing a volume similar in form to the *Collections* of the Massachusetts Historical Society. Chaired by Henry Barnard, it recommended as the topic of the first volume "a documentary history of the Society" but, lacking sufficient funds, nothing came of this first proposal. Although the Society was not in a position to assume the financial burden of publishing its own *Collections* until 1860, several works were printed "under the patronage of the Society," including a small genealogical magazine which appeared in two numbers, and two lectures delivered before the Society in the 1840s. A Publications Committee was formed in 1850 and recommended that John W. DeForest's useful *History of Connecticut Indians* be published under the Society's name. In 1855, a change in the by-laws provided that the proceeds of a legacy left by Thomas Day, the fees of life members, and special donations and subscriptions would be employed to pay for the expense of an annual volume, *Journal and Contributions of the Connecticut Historical Society.*

The 15 years following the revival of the Society were enormously fruitful in the development of the collections, in the promotion of historical awareness, and in the solution of practical problems of existence. But with the deaths of Thomas Day in 1855 and Thomas Robbins in 1856, an important era in the life of the Historical Society drew to a close. There were a number of charter members of the organization still alive, but none were very active at this point. Leadership was efficiently assumed, indeed had already passed, to experienced men like Henry Barnard and Charles and James Hosmer. The influence of still younger men like James Hammond Trumbull was already being felt. Both Day and Robbins left sums of money to the Society, creating the beginnings of an endowment that was to steadily grow. More important, each in their way had established models of dedicated service that would inspire a new generation of officers and members.

A Period of Stability
1855–1890

DURING THE YEARS FROM 1839 to 1855, the essential framework of The Connecticut Historical Society was erected; in the following 35 years, work continued within the established outline. The accomplishments of this period were solid achievements, less dramatic perhaps than those which preceded them, but important nonetheless. Annual meetings were held in May, when officers were elected, the Treasurer's report read, and the year's accomplishments measured. Twice-monthly meetings gave way in 1849 to monthly sessions held on the first Tuesday of the month which has been the rule ever since. For several years, in the 1840s and 1850s, the regular meetings were supplemented by a special lecture and entertainment series. After 1856, they were abandoned and papers were typically presented during the regular monthly gatherings. The average turnout for those sessions during the nineteenth century was not large, despite a fairly sizeable membership. The difficulties of transportation for members scattered all over the State were such that attendance for those beyond the immediate vicinity of Hartford was rare. During the winter months, when weather was stormy, it was sometimes difficult to secure the quorum necessary for the conduct of business. The advantage of those small turnouts, however, was a friendliness and an ease of communication that is hard to preserve with much larger groups.

Collecting for the Cabinet and Library continued as before, but outright purchases by the Society were rare. Although Thomas Robbins occasionally purchased items offered to the institution by convincing members to subscribe for that purpose, the growth of the Library had to depend on the gifts of friends and supporters. Thus the development of the book collections tended to reflect the interests of the various donors. The addition of Thomas Robbins's library brought to the Society a clergyman's collection, a rich assortment of sermons, theological treatises, as well as general historical works and a fine assortment of early English folios. Other contributors, following the program presented by Thomas Day in 1839, contributed bound volumes of newspapers, family genealogies, memoirs and Connecticut imprints. Institutions were especially helpful, forwarding to Hartford their annual proceedings, catalogs and assorted monographs. The interest and contributions of astute bookmen like James Hammond Trumbull, Charles J. Hoadly and the noted collector George Brinley insured that items of Connecticut interest would at least be considered by one or more members of the institution. Henry Stevens of Vermont and London, the remarkable book dealer, became a member and performed many services as well as making valuable donations.

Between 1839 and 1854, the library collection circulated among members. A small bound volume labeled "books loaned" and arranged by borrower provides an indication of the reading preferences of members as well as evidence that loans were not always promptly returned. Rules were adopted in 1845 that no books or pamphlets were to be removed without the permission of the Librarian. Four weeks were allowed for loans and overdue fines of 25¢ a week were to be assessed. Security was an additional problem, prompting the Library Committee in 1849 to exclude children from the Society's rooms unless accompanied by an adult. The nuisance continued, for on March 8, 1850, Thomas Robbins wrote in his diary, "Have concluded to exclude boys without protection from my room. Have had losses, a considerable number, and some valuable." There may well have been more systematic plundering, for in 1851 Charles Hosmer complained that pamphlets "taken in an irregular manner" from the rooms of the Society had turned up in the library of the New-York Historical Society. All of these considerations played a part in the decision of 1854 to repeal the regulation allowing books to circulate. To the Society's great credit, however, all qualified readers were admitted to the Reading Room and, in special cases, books were loaned upon written application to the Standing Committee.

What is now considered the museum collection of the Society also grew steadily, yet here there was a different perspective in the approach taken to acquisition. Books, pamphlets and manuscripts may have a sentimental aspect to them, particularly when they are inscribed by or written in the hand of a notable figure but, even to the most uncritical eye, they have always been, primarily, sources for information. Not so the costume, the contemporary portrait, the sword or musket. These may serve as evidence for such general questions as the nature of taste, the character of weaponry, or the physical appearance of an historical figure, but when they were collected by the Historical Society in the nineteenth century, they were regarded with almost religious veneration. To Thomas Robbins they were "sacred things." The term *relic* was used repeatedly to refer to what we now call museum objects, and that expression accurately conveys the sense of awe in which they were held. The relic brought the viewer into an almost physical contact with the distant hero or heroine and imparted, or seemed to, some of his or her qualities to the viewer.

In time our attitude toward these objects has become more detached, more critical and objective, making collecting more selective, analytical and dispassionate. When the transition to a more scientific view of historical artifacts began is difficult to determine. Certainly the presentation of the bloodied shirt of Colonel William Ledyard in 1841 and the battle sword of General Israel Putnam in 1859 were opportunities for moving

One of the treasured "relics" of the Society, the battle sword of General Israel Putnam, presented in 1859

ceremonies at the rooms of the Society, evoking past heroism. On the other hand, one of the consequences of this emotional approach to collecting was the accumulation of a miscellaneous assortment both of important objects and minor items of trivia. Pieces of an Egyptian pyramid, worn shingles from an early house, along with one "queen bee" were to be found at the Society along with important, documented pieces of furniture, signed paintings and marked pieces of silver. Indiscriminate collections in other historical societies provoked several directors to close up their museums entirely, depositing their relics at other institutions. It is fortunate that The Connecticut Historical Society has retained a bit of the sense of awe towards its historical relics and has refused to eliminate its museum, despite the fact that adequate funds and staff were lacking for many years for their effective care. Today, the associations that once made certain objects worthy of veneration serve to document and authenticate them. Sensible deposits in other institutions of collections peripheral to Connecticut history have made it easier to maintain, classify and interpret those that remain.

Whether it is eighteenth-century imprints or pieces of Puritan furniture, collection and preservation is only the first step for an historical society; the next is systematic arrangement which is necessary if the collection is to be consulted. The Connecticut Historical Society acted promptly to make its printed and manuscript collections available to qualified readers, though it lagged, understandably, in its treatment of museum pieces. Visitors to the Society called again and again for adequate labeling of the relics on display. After the death of Thomas Robbins there was no one on hand each day to repeat the tales connected with each object on view. Only in the last 25 years, in fact, has there been adequate staff and sufficient expertise to fully identify, document, and arrange the varied collection of prints, paintings, tools, furniture and decorative objects in the Society's possession.

The Library received the bulk of the attention in the early days. An accessions book was begun in 1839, pamphlets were gathered together and bound, and the important manuscript collections were pasted into folio volumes. Some of this work was fairly crude by today's standards and eventually had to be undone, but a beginning was made. The construction of a book catalog, arranged by author and title, was commenced under Thomas Robbins who employed several assistants to carry on the work, but progress was necessarily slow. Aside from the expense, one major difficulty was that the catalog was not keyed to the location of the book. For shelving books, a system of categories had to be developed and the Dewey decimal system, first proposed in 1876, was eventually adopted by the Society for the cataloging of its books in 1946.

Due to Thomas Robbins's increasing frailty, the Library of the Society, at the time of his death in 1856, was in a state of confusion. Many books were simply piled on the floor and the catalog was far from complete. Moreover, there were serious doubts among the members whether the Society could afford to replace Robbins, and for nearly a year its Historical Rooms at the Atheneum were kept open by a Miss Jane Root. At the annual meeting of May 26, 1857, Frederick Beecher Perkins, a Hartford native and a Yale graduate, was elected to the position left vacant at Robbins's death at a salary of $60 a month. There is some confusion, however, about precisely how long he served as the Society's Librarian. He was not re-elected to the post at the next annual meeting, nor was his salary paid after his first year. On May 15, 1858, Perkins submitted a report summarizing his accomplishments of the previous year, while the Library Committee, headed by Henry Barnard, presented its own report. Frederick Perkins pointed out that the bulk of his labor had been spent in compiling a catalog consisting of two indices, an author and a short-title list. The Library Committee generally supported Perkins's report, differing seriously, however, in its estimate of the cost of the work he had performed. The Committee nonetheless called upon the members to appoint a Librarian as soon as money could be found, for Henry Barnard, author of the report, argued that the Library was not yet as accessible to the community, nor "as honorable to the Society as it ought to be."

At the annual meeting, held on May 21, 1858, it was voted "unanimously, that it is inexpedient at this time, to appoint a Librarian for the Connecticut Historical Society." On June 1,

1858, it was agreed by the Standing Committee that the cataloging labors of Frederick Perkins "which he had commenced as Librarian" could, "by the aid of voluntary subscriptions, be completed without further expense to the Society." One or more benefactors apparently provided the funds to enable Perkins to continue, for a short time, his work of arranging and cataloging the Library.

Frederick Perkins continued to serve the Library in an informal way until 1861, but all responsibility for the book collection finally had to be assumed by the Library Committee. The rooms of the Society were turned over to the care of Miss Root who remained on as custodian until 1876 when she was replaced by a Miss Morgan. While the decision not to fill the position of Librarian was undoubtedly a sound financial one, allowing more of the funds available to be invested in the permanent fund, it also left the institution without the kind of day-to-day leadership and management that is vital to continued expansion.

The 1860s brought a marked improvement in the physical setting of the Historical Society. David Watkinson, a successful Hartford businessman and philanthropist, died in 1857, leaving in his will a substantial sum to various worthy causes, including $100,000 "for the purpose of establishing in connection with the Connecticut Historical Society a library of reference, to be accessible at all reasonable hours and times to all citizens and other residents and visitors in the State of Connecticut." Of that sum, $5,000 was to be used to build an addition to The Connecticut Historical Society which would also house the new "library of reference." Another fund of $15,000 was to be set aside, the income from which was to be used for the salary of a librarian to be appointed by the Historical Society with the approval of the Watkinson Library trustees. An act of incorporation was secured in May, 1858 and the purchase of land adjacent to the Wadsworth Atheneum was completed in December. In April of 1862, the Historical Society, acting through a committee consisting of Calvin Day, Erastus Smith and James Hammond Trumbull, began to consider various plans for an addition to the Atheneum. Architectural drawings of the approved plan were soon put on public view as announced in the *Courant* of April 23:

The design of the new building for the Watkinson Library is exhibited in Hemingway & Stevens' show window. It is a good thing, and you must see it. Description will not do it justice. O. J. Jordan was the architect.

Another article in the same issue of the *Courant* noted that the stockholders of the Wadsworth confirmed the vote of the directors permitting the Historical Society to proceed with the construction, adding:

> If the Historical Society needs anything, it is an additional room. The valuable and curious collection is now in a terrible jumble, and thrown together without regard to regularity. A larger room, well arranged goods and something somewhere to tell what a thing is when you see it, and then the Historical Museum will be a place to tie up to.

On May 14, 1862 an agreement was reached between The Connecticut Historical Society and the trustees of the Watkinson in which each institution agreed to form "a perpetual union" to carry forward the purposes of David Watkinson's will. The Historical Society agreed to construct the addition that would house the library of reference, as well as provide additional space for its own collections, with the provision that the older institution could take over in the future the entire space upon adequate notice to and equal compensation for the Watkinson. Thus it was anticipated that the "perpetual union" might, under certain circumstances, be dissolved.

In 1863, when the question of appointing a joint Librarian came up, the officers of the Historical Society concluded that the institution could not afford either to set aside the principal sum of $15,000 or contribute $1,000 annually for the purpose. The right to appoint a Librarian for the younger institution was suspended with the hope that it might be exercised at some later point in time. Though there was disappointment in that decision, there was compensation in the added room provided for the Society and in the close working relationship which developed between the two organizations sharing what was then called "library hall." As James Hammond Trumbull

James Hammond Trumbull (1821–1897), President of the Society, 1863–1889, painted by William R. Wheeler in 1880

explained in 1876, "for the purposes of consultation, the Watkinson and the Historical Society's libraries are virtually one, with an aggregate of about forty-three thousand volumes."

The gap left by the death of Robbins could only be partially bridged by the remaining members. No one appeared on the scene with quite the same single-minded devotion to the affairs of the institution. If anything, Hartford was too dense at mid-century in clubs, institutes and societies to allow any one of them to absorb the energies of all its members. Even Henry Barnard, one of the most active members, asked, in 1860, to be relieved from all official positions. He was, in fact, to continue for many years as Vice-President, but the request was symptomatic of the pressures caused by rival commitments.

That progress continued at all during those years without a Librarian is largely due to two men, James Hammond Trumbull (1821–1897) and Charles Jeremy Hoadly (1828–1900). Elected a member in 1847, Trumbull was selected as Cor-

Charles Jeremy Hoadly (1828–1900), Corresponding Secretary of the Society, 1863–1890, President, 1894–1900, painted by Charles Noel Flagg in 1898

responding Secretary in 1848 and as President in 1863, a position he held until 1889. Charles J. Hoadly, succeeding Trumbull as Corresponding Secretary and filling that office until 1890, was also President of the Society from 1894 until his death in 1900. Men of contrasting physical types, they were alike in their fastidious scholarship, their professional pride and their sense of personal dignity. Inevitably they were rivals: Henry Allen Castle, elected a member in 1894, remembered that when the two men attended meetings, neither "gave evidence of brotherly love for the other." Trumbull had the reputation of being one of the few men who could read Eliot's Indian Bible, but when Castle mentioned that to Hoadly, he retorted, "Humph. He says he can."

Both men came from old Connecticut stock and grew up in a similar atmosphere of family pride. Governor Jonathan Trumbull had invited James Hammond Trumbull's grandfather down from Massachusetts to establish a newspaper in

Norwich in 1773. Trumbull's father continued as editor, participated in the defense of Stonington against the British in 1814, and later became a successful merchant, still finding time to become an authority on local history. Charles Hoadly was a descendant of William Hoadly, one of the first settlers of Branford, and a grandson of Jeremy Hoadley, Mayor, selectman and representative from Hartford in the General Assembly. The proud owner of the original manuscript coat-of-arms to the English Hoadleys, it was characteristic of Charles Hoadly's stubborn attachment to the ways of the past that he insisted on returning to the earliest English spelling of his surname.

Both Trumbull and Hoadly were born into politically active, Whig families. They were intitially inclined towards the law, but were eventually drawn, by a stronger interest, to parallel careers as scholar-librarians. Trumbull was in his third year at Yale in 1840 when ill health forced him to return to Stonington to regain his strength. There he pursued the study of natural history, collecting and classifying all the shells he could find or acquire. He entered into correspondence with James Linsley, a member of Yale's Natural History Society, providing Linsley with the results of his investigations. While Trumbull's catalogs, written out in a meticulous hand, reveal a strong urge to order and classify the random facts of nature, his interest in history was never lost. In 1841 he toured New England, visiting antiquarian book stores in Boston, making copies of early documents at the State House in Hartford, and visiting the room of the Historical Society where he impressed Charles Hosmer with an historical knowledge surprising in a youth of 20. In 1847 he was invited by Henry Barnard to assist Thomas Robbins, a position he was prepared to accept when he was offered the more tempting post of Assistant Secretary of the State. On his own time, Trumbull began to arrange and transcribe the more important documents under his charge, eventually publishing three volumes of the *Public Records of the Colony of Connecticut* covering the years from 1639 to 1689. Appointed the first State Librarian in 1854, he served again as Assistant Secretary of the State from 1858 to 1861 and as Secretary of the State from 1861 to 1865. In 1863 he was appointed Librarian of the Watkinson Library which allowed him to work closely with The Connecticut Historical Society.

After graduation from Trinity College in 1851, Hoadly, on the other hand, entered the office of Henry Barnard, then Superintendent of Public Instruction, and at the same time began the study of law. In 1854 he was appointed Librarian of Trinity and in the following year was admitted to the Bar. Hoadly never entered the legal profession for in April, 1855 he succeeded Trumbull as State Librarian. There he remained for the next 43 years, guiding the growth of the State Library and editing the next 15 volumes of the *Public Records*.

Both Trumbull and Hoadly were prolific scholars with national reputations. Charles Hoadly's bibliography lists 44 items all connected with Connecticut history. Among James Hammond Trumbull's more important historical contributions were the catalog of the George Brinley library, his checklist of eighteenth-century Connecticut imprints, and his two-volume *Memorial History of Hartford County*. Trumbull's interests extended further, however, and the list of his memberships— founding member of both the American Philological Society and the American Oriental Society, and an elected member of the National Academy of Sciences, among others—reflects a wide-ranging intellect. Yet Trumbull and Hoadly were curiously alike in the character of their work; they were most at home in dealing with technical historical problems, and they were both fond of exploding historical myths. According to one account, Hoadly "occupied himself with the minute details of severely restricted fields of historical and legal investigation; preferring rather to work therein with care and accuracy than to treat larger subjects with brilliant inexactness." Of Trumbull it was later said that he "might have given us a history of Connecticut that would have stood first among American histories." His reluctance to paint on a large historical canvas was attributed, it was suggested, to a fear of contradiction and criticism.

It might be added that both men came to maturity in a period when historical writing was beginning a transition away from the impressionistic and often careless style of the romantic era. Neither was trained in any formal sense for historical research—the age of graduate schools conducted with Teutonic thoroughness was a generation away—and yet both men anticipated the methodical, scientific approach that came to prevail among academic historians of a later period.

The more methodical approach to history was accompanied by a slight shift from the attitude of strict veneration for the past which had marked the first generation of the Society's members. James Hammond Trumbull, for example, believed that the study of history in the schools should begin with local history, but he insisted that interpretation rather than memorization should be emphasized. He was not inclined, as Thomas Robbins had been, to absolve the early settlers of New England of all blame in their treatment of the Indians. When he was questioned about a memorial to the Pequot War, he replied that, in his judgment, the monument should be "primarily *historical* rather than *triumphal*"; the design, he insisted, "should commemorate the event and not honor the victory," adding "the history of the Pequot War is not the chapter of our colonial history which I want to remember with most pride."

In an unpublished essay dating from the 1860s (judging solely from internal evidence), James Hammond Trumbull described with rare psychological insight the mixed feelings of one who felt proud of his ancestors while being acutely aware at the same time of living in an age of continual improvement and change. In admiring our ancestors, he wrote, we indulge our egos. "It is hardly less pleasant," he confessed, "to be proud of one's ancestors than of one's self." The departed forefather, he added playfully, "only had a life estate in his greatness." The more we can establish his title to greatness, Trumbull continued, the more secure is the inheritance for subsequent generations:

So we sacredly guard the relics of the olden time,—and form historical societies,—and set Dr. Dryasdust at work,—and cultivate our genealogical trees,—and point to Stuyvesant's tobacco pipe or Miles Standish's sword with the same conscious pride with which the old warder of Norwich castle displays the capacious dinner pot or the gigantic helmet of the redoubtable Guy.

· 53 ·

Trumbull brought the same humorous touch to his second theme, the conviction of living in an age of progress. Just as widespread as the reverence for antiquity, he wrote, is the belief that "we ourselves, as a generation, are wiser, smarter, better, and *better* off than any generation which has preceded us on the world's stage." Even "the most rigid conservative, the most reverent worshipper of the past," he insisted, would inevitably be affected by the current mood of optimism and progress. Trumbull's solution to the dilemma was the rhetorical device of turning to the image of the dwarf who climbs up an old fig tree in order to see farther and gain superior vision "by deliberate comparison or contrast of what has been with what is." A delightful stylist and a man of fine wit, it is regrettable that Trumbull avoided the broad synthesis in favor of specific topics.

The contributions of Hoadly and Trumbull to the Historical Society were many : they held, over a period of 40 years, the most important offices of the Society; they sat together on all the important committees; and they both deserve credit for the first three volumes of the *Collections of the Connecticut Historical Society* published in 1860, 1870 and 1895. Hoadly edited the first and third volumes, Trumbull the second and, in the persistently high quality of their editorial work, they established standards for others to emulate. In addition, their lectures before the members and guests of the institution provided many informative evenings. Neither man was markedly wealthy, but the Society benefitted from the personal collections of books and manuscripts that were later donated by their heirs. Both men admittedly served other institutions— Hoadly, the State Library; and, Trumbull, the Watkinson Library—but they devoted as much of their free time and wisdom as they were able to the Historical Society.

There were two innovations adopted during the age of Hoadly and Trumbull which rendered the Society a more congenial institution. With the election of Miss Ellen D. Larned of Thompson, the noted historian of Windham County, it ceased to be a strictly masculine institution, yet for 20 years Miss Larned remained a lonely representative of her sex on the membership rolls, and there is no evidence that she

The annual "field day" on June 5, 1888 led to this group photograph at the Pequot battle ground in Mystic

was able to attend more than an occasional meeting. It was not until 1890, when four ladies were elected, that she was joined in force and the masculine tone of the institution was softened. The female presence was immediately felt: in May, 1890 Miss Larned was elected a Vice-President, a position she continued to hold until 1912; in the next decades many lectures were delivered by women members; of note, too, is the fact that Mary Kingsbury Talcott, one of the best genealogists of her day, edited the Talcott papers for the fourth volume of the *Collections* published in 1892.

The second innovation in the changing organization was the annual "field day." In June of 1888, the Society began a series of annual outings that was to last until 1897. A group of members and guests would generally gather at the Hartford railroad station, board a special car, and proceed in high spirits to a stop near one of several historic sites. From that stop they usually continued by carriage to their destination where one of the members, or a local antiquarian, would lead a guided tour. The festive party would then repair to a hotel for a meal punctuated with toasts to their hosts and pleasant speeches. In successive years, members visited Mystic, Deerfield, Plymouth, Lebanon, Salem, Windsor, Lexington and Concord, New London and Groton, with the more distant expeditions extending over two days. It was on the trip to New London that Jonathan F. Morris remarked dryly that he had discovered the remains of the Saybrook Platform.

Individuals had been making such pilgrimages since the youth of Thomas Robbins. Benson J. Lossing's guide to the sites of the American Revolution had been a bestseller of the 1850s. The erection of countless monuments at the location of heroic episodes was designed not only to commemorate those events but also to provide beacons to guide visitors. The organized outings of the Historical Society reflected the growing urge to travel in an America that was growing increasingly urban and industrial. Those trips expressed as well the desire to experience directly the total setting of an event, whether it was felt through the old houses of Deerfield, the terrain around Pequot Fort, or the atmosphere of Plymouth Harbor. There is no evidence to explain why the field days were abandoned after 1897, but they were much enjoyed while they lasted.

The days of the Society without a Librarian came to an end in 1879 with the employment of William Isaac Fletcher. After a "common school" education and a training in bibliography under W. F. Poole at the Boston Atheneum, Fletcher became Librarian of the Silas Bronson Library in Waterbury. He returned to Massachusetts but was later attracted to Hartford by the prospect of working under Trumbull at the Watkinson Library. Until 1883, when he left to become the Librarian of Amherst College, Fletcher served half-time for the two institutions sharing the "historical hall" of the Atheneum. While with the Society, he worked on the author catalog and initiated the annual report of the Librarian in which he listed new accessions, the number of readers, and such proposals as seemed desirable.

After Fletcher's departure in 1883, the Society elected Frank Butler Gay to become its new Librarian and Recording Secretary. He was born in East Granby in 1856 of a family that traced its ancestors back to early settlers of Hartford. After a well-rounded secondary education in the liberal arts, Gay went to work at the offices of the *Courant* before joining the Hartford Library Association as an assistant under Caroline Maria Hewins. In 1883 he came to the Atheneum to assist James Hammond Trumbull as well as to replace Fletcher at the Historical Society. Under the watchful eye of Trumbull, Gay secured an excellent training in the discriminating skills of bibliography. In 1890, when Trumbull retired from his position at the Watkinson, Frank Gay was named Acting Librarian in his place. After two years of dividing his time between the two libraries, he resigned his position at the Historical Society. During his tenure he had done his best to awaken interest in the institution and to establish some degree of order in the collections. The odds he faced were severe, as his last report in May, 1892 would indicate:

> With all the means of gratulation—and there have never been more in any year of the Society's history—the evident and pressing need of more funds, a trained assistant, more interest and work from among the members is very apparent. . . . Owing to cramped quarters, lack of funds and competent assistance, this library has not entirely succeeded in its public functions. Although rich in manuscript collections, it has been impossible to consult them. With the cases, shelves, drawers, boxes, and cupboards, fairly bursting with their contents of books, pamphlets, and papers, without a classified arrangement or catalogue, a large part of the library has been practically useless.

It was not the most diplomatic Librarian's message on record, but Frank Gay probably knew he would shortly be hanging up one of his two hats.

One of Gay's last major decisions was to hire a young man from East Granby, Albert Carlos Bates, to assist him in shifting books and manuscripts prior to a rearrangement of space in the Atheneum. "Mr. Bates," declared Gay in that otherwise pessimistic report, "has some exceptional qualities which fit him for this work, and the Society was fortunate in securing him." The Society was equally fortunate in retaining him. Elected the institutions's fifth Librarian in January, 1893, Albert Bates held that position continually until his retirement in May of 1940. During that remarkable tenure, and due in large measure to his continued energy and discipline, the effectiveness of the Society, its ability to perform what Gay called its "public functions," steadily increased. For that reason the next period in the history of the Society, from 1893 to 1940, may properly be called the era of Albert Carlos Bates.

The Era of Albert Carlos Bates
1890–1940

ALBERT CARLOS BATES, like his older friend and neighbor, Frank Gay, was born and raised in East Granby, Connecticut. An accomplished genealogist, an officer in the Bates Family Association and a member of the Connecticut Sons of the American Revolution, Albert Bates worked up, in the 1890s, a sketch of his ancestors which was eventually published in the 1940s. He was a direct descendant of John Bates of Lydd, England and Lemuel Bates (1729–1803), a large landowner and successful farmer who had settled in Turkey Hills (later East Granby) in the 1760s. The house that Lemuel built in 1773 was occupied, at the time Bates wrote his sketch, by the fifth generation of descendants. The eighteenth century and the events of the Revolution were never remote to Albert Bates. Lemuel was a Captain in the Connecticut militia during the Revolution; Erastus Bates, Albert's grandfather, was born in 1764 and was commissioned a Lieutenant in the militia in 1799; Albert's father was born in 1808 and was thus in his old age when his son was entering school. Albert Carlos Bates's special respect for the past was closely connected to the experience of growing up with older parents in an atmosphere of intense family pride. Later in life, he told his assistant, Mary Helen Kidder, that it was his mother who encouraged his interest in Connecticut by telling him stories that could not be found in published sources. The family attic, with its old books, almanacs, and the large chest "containing files of old newspapers, bundles of

Albert Carlos Bates (1865–1954), Librarian of the Society, 1892–1940, painted by James Goodwin McManus in 1925

letters, and other written papers" also had much to do with stimulating an interest in the past.

From his father and grandfather Albert also acquired the habits and instincts of the proverbial Yankee trader. In his introduction to some of Albert Bates's recollections, Thompson R. Harlow has written that he was "as shrewd a collector as ever came on the market." The Granby native came by it naturally, perhaps, describing. his grandfather as "much given to trading, thus showing he was a true Yankee." Carlos Bates, Albert's father, kept a general store for a time, travelled extensively as a collector of bills for a clock manufacturer, and later in life "attended to much business of others, settling numerous estates, both of insolvents and of deceased persons." The inheritance of business skills proved useful to the Historical Society for only a man with the instincts of a "true Yankee" could have managed, during a period when the Society's budget could

. 60 .

barely cover salaries, to secure so many treasures for so little money.

From childhood, Albert Bates was drawn to Hartford's libraries, often visiting the Hartford Library Association where Caroline M. Hewins presided or, more frequently, the Watkinson, to see Mr. Gay. In 1885 Bates graduated from the Connecticut Literary Institution in Suffield and returned to work on the family farm. In April of 1892 Frank Gay asked him if he would assist in shifting materials in anticipation of another relocation of the Society within the Atheneum building. Here follows Albert Bates's own recollections of his first months of service:

> I began my duties with the Society Monday, May 2nd, 1892, reserving Saturdays for my own work at home as Town Clerk and Treasurer that year. I took care of my horse, milked the cow and drove the six miles to Windsor Locks, boarding the 7:32 train, returning at night on the train leaving, I believe, exactly at six. This continued until it came dark so early that it was difficult to find the cow on my return home, and I then arranged with the next door neighbor to care for the cow and supply our home with milk. I continued this daily travel through the year, reaching Windsor Locks about sunrise in the latter part of December. Before the end of the year, I was offered the position of Librarian which I accepted, and commenced my duties with the beginning of 1893.

The Society had a new Librarian and Albert Bates, at the age of 27, had a new career.

The relocation of the Historical Society at this time was but a small part of a larger reorganization of the institutions sheltered within the Atheneum. By 1880 it had become increasingly clear that Hartford needed a public library with open circulation accessible to the entire community. The Atheneum's art gallery was a dark and confusing maze of pictures and sculptures, and both the Watkinson Library and the Historical Society needed additional space to house their collections. Committees from both the Historical Society and the

Watkinson were formed to explore various solutions to the problem. A joint committee of all the organizations within the Atheneum building resolved, on March 17, 1882, "that a more intimate connection of the Institutions we represent, for the purpose of establishing a Free Public Library and a Free Art Gallery, would if practicable, greatly promote the public good and the ends for which these Institutions were severally founded." A committee of four representing each organization was established to draw up "a plan of union." The *Courant* waxed euphoric at the vision of a single cultural complex housed at the Atheneum under one extensive roof:

> The possibilities, which such a proposition opens up, are vast. Comparatively few of our own citizens know the full value of the books gathered under the roof of the Atheneum building; the rich associations that gather around the many interesting objects in the Historical Society's keeping; the real artistic merit of many of the paintings and works of sculpture in the art gallery, or the extent and diversity of the Hartford subscription library.

The practicality of the proposed union was increased in March of 1883 when the General Assembly passed a special act authorizing the City of Hartford to appropriate part of its income to the grand plan, but the difficulties in the path of absolute union were quickly perceived. The Historical Society, the Watkinson Library, the Gallery of Art and the Hartford Library Association were separate corporate bodies with distinct resources, rights and legal obligations. Working out a solution involved, in the words of one observer, "much searching of hearts and cudgelling of brains." Those who wish to follow the protracted course of negotiations should read Marian G. M. Clarke's excellent study of the Watkinson Library. The reorganization required that the Historical Society, the Watkinson and the Library Association convey to the Wadsworth Atheneum their property rights in the Atheneum building. The final solution saw the Library Association transformed into a public library and the Wadsworth Atheneum declared a public art gallery. The Watkinson Library and the Historical Society were to remain within the Atheneum, but were now to be located in separate parts of the building. Frank Gay, whose time was divided between the two institutions, no longer felt he could serve both organizations, and Albert Bates entered as the Historical Society's Librarian. To alleviate the problems of overcrowding a new addition had to be constructed for the Watkinson, and the Historical Society would then be able to take over the released space. A campaign was begun in 1890 to raise $400,000 in contributions from the people of Hartford to finance the new addition, and in January of 1893 the enlarged quarters were unveiled to the public.

The condition of the Historical Society at the time of the reorganization was discouraging to many of its supporters. The institution's financial state placed severe limitations on its ability to acquire materials and hire sufficient staff to make the collections accessible. During the decade of the 1890s, the annual budget hovered around the modest level of $1,800. Half of the Society's income was derived from dividends and interest, the remainder from membership fees and dues. There were to be several campaigns to increase the membership rolls in order to increase income, but deficits were frequent and had to be covered by special subscriptions. The salary of the Librarian absorbed fully two-thirds of the income, leaving only one-third for the expense of keeping the rooms open. The Society's book fund, established by Lucy A. Brainard with a gift of $100, had been started in the hopes that others would contribute, but the response was disheartening and for some time the lack of funds to purchase new genealogies and local histories was a matter of grave concern.

At the time that Albert Bates was hired, it was decided to merge the office of Custodian with that of Librarian. Consequently, his energy was distributed very widely indeed and inevitably the Librarian's effectiveness was reduced. During one severe illness in 1895, an assistant, Alice M. Gay, was hired to keep the rooms open, but not until 1928 was the Society able to afford a full-time assistant. The usefulness of the Library was further curtailed by the shortage of money, the pressing need for additional shelf space, and by inadequate cataloging. The small number of readers reflected the disorder that prevailed. In six months of 1880, a scant 75 readers consulted the collections, while in 1884–1885 Frank Gay could only report 190 readers. For lack of space, some books were stored with the Watkinson's collections, others had to be piled on the floor, making the retrieval of books for patrons difficult. Any experienced librarian would have been rapidly discouraged, but, fortunately, Albert Bates in 1893 was young, energetic, and indifferent to the prospect of work at any place but the Historical Society.

Historically-minded, Bates was nonetheless untrained as a librarian and he had to master the basic skills of his new profession. He began by arranging the manuscript collections, most of which had never been sorted, collated or described. Valuable documents turned up in the oddest places; he found, for instance, "the early deed of Saybrook . . . lying on the top of a tall case, . . . covered by a quarter of an inch of dust." Nathan Hale's diary was discovered among a group of papers that once belonged to Isaac W. Stuart; and, an important map of Connecticut was found "crushed in a bundle in the cupboard under one of the cases in our hall." After arranging them, he began "listing some of them on a catalogue," later explaining in his recollections that his first attempts at cataloging could best be described as mere "listing." Bates also spent his evenings in the Library reading the manuscripts that he had arranged during the day. With the aid of Frank Gay and Reverend William DeLoss Love, Chairman of the Library Committee, his bibliographical skills improved rapidly, and he was soon compiling a checklist of Connecticut session laws, aided by the Society's first typewriter—a model that had been fortuitously left for trial by a salesman but was never picked up.

Albert Bates's usefulness to the Society steadily increased. In 1896 he was elected Recording Secretary, and in the same year delivered his first scholarly paper on the Connecticut Gore Land Company. In addition to his duties as Librarian, he gradually assumed the Society's editorial responsibilities, beginning with proofreading, moving on to the selection and editing of documents, and improving on preceding editorial

One of the discoveries of 1893, a confirmatory Indian deed dated 1666, in which Uncas, the Mohegan Sachem, and his wife and three sons, Sunk Squaw, Oneco, Joshua and Amatha (each with pictographic signatures), reaffirmed the sale of lands to the people of Saybrook

practice by retaining original spelling and punctuation. According to Bates, his most difficult task was compiling a list of probate districts. He consulted Charles J. Hoadly on the matter who told him that he had once made such a list only to loan it out to someone who never returned it. This was the only information that Hoadly offered, and Albert Bates felt that he was being tested. If he was, he passed with reputation enhanced as only two errors subsequently came to light.

Identifying priorities and arriving at what today would be

called an "acquisitions program" was probably Albert Bates's most significant contribution. It was only with purposeful book buying that the modest income of the Society could be employed effectively. It is true that he had certain interests— Indian artifacts, coins and medals, for example—that are no longer considered as important as they were in the past. He was unwilling to refuse gifts even when they were clearly inappropriate to the purposes of the Society. Unfortunately, there has not been, until the last 35 years, adequate clarity or sufficient definition in the development of the museum collections, but Albert Bates did move rapidly to define what sorts of books and manuscripts the Society should be acquiring, and he defined priorities so well that the development of the Library has continued within the outlines he prescribed.

The Historical Society had been established for the purpose of collecting the materials of national as well as Connecticut history. The pretense of assembling a national collection was decisively left behind during this period and the concentration came to rest squarely on Connecticut sources. In the "rare book" field Bates concentrated on Connecticut imprints, carefully building up the Society's collection. Each year in his annual report, he announced the number of eighteenth-century imprints acquired by the Society in the previous 12 months. He also systematically improved the collection of Connecticut newspapers, understanding fully the value imparted by those important sources. He was equally interested in collecting manuscripts bearing on Connecticut history, though the Society had to depend on the generosity of individual members when important items came on the market. He also felt it was important to maintain the strength of the genealogical collection, and he appended to the *Annual Report* of 1894 a list of all printed and manuscript genealogies in the Society's Library. Under his prompting a subscription was raised to purchase the D. Williams Patterson library, a substantial collection of family histories.

His profound interest in the history of printing in Connecticut was reflected in the crucial part Albert Bates played in organizing the Acorn Club, founded in 1899 for the purpose of "issuing either as reprints or as original publications rare printed books or early manuscripts especially relating to Connecticut." It appears to have been modelled after the Club of Odd Volumes started in Boston for similar purposes in 1887. Bates was Editor of the Acorn Club from 1899 to 1906, during which time it published his *Connecticut Statute Laws* and James Hammond Trumbull's *List of Books Printed in Connecticut, 1709–1800* (a work which Bates had to put together from manuscript slips left to Trumbull's daughter, Annie Eliot Trumbull). In his introduction to Trumbull's work, he noted some of the weaknesses of the compilation: abbreviated titles, omission in many cases of the name of the printer, inconsistent punctuation, and the absence of collations, but his criticisms were those of a fellow bibliographer who understood that standards of description had changed considerably in the 40 years since the first entries were written. Scientific bibliography was taking shape only at the turn of the century and he was part of the movement connected with the emergence of this discipline. Bates was clearly optimistic that he could improve on Trumbull's bibliography and in his introduction to the checklist, the Historical Society's Librarian requested readers who discovered unidentified titles or editions to forward "a full copy of its title and imprint with its collation" to any member of the Acorn Club.

Trumbull's list included 1,741 entries of books and pamphlets printed in Connecticut before 1801. In 1938 Albert Bates and the Acorn Club published its first supplementary list, bringing the total number of imprints before 1801 to 2,820. It may be noted that half of those additions were missing in Charles Evans's *American Bibliography* (volumes 1–12, 1903–1934). Another supplement compiled by Bates appeared in 1947 and brought the total number of recorded Connecticut imprints to 2,903. In notes attached to the text, Bates pointed out that to this number might be added 355 identified statutes, over 1,650 Connecticut broadsides, and some 60 Fast and Thanksgiving proclamations, undiscovered but undoubtedly printed. With a small allowance for a few titles yet to be discovered, he thought the total number of imprints for the State easily exceeded 5,000 for the period. Bates took pride in the achievement of eighteen-century printers, concluding that "this is a remarkable record for ninety-two years of industry by the printers of the small state of Connecticut." In his day Albert Bates, like James Hammond Trumbull before him, was Connecticut's foremost bibliographer and, as Librarian of the Historical Society, it was his goal to assemble as many of those 5,000 titles as he could. Today, the Historical Society owns approximately 70% of that number, with certainly the largest number of unique Connecticut items held by any institution.

Absorbed as he was by the problems of scholarship, Albert Bates also had to manage the day-to-day affairs of the Society. He paid bills, answered genealogical questions, led tours and carried books for patrons, but there is evidence that his patience occasionally wore thin. He objected to queries mailed to the Society without stamps for their replies and he disliked performing merely routine genealogical research. Sometimes he requested a token payment before he would supply the needed information, though he gradually fell into the habit of recommending professional researchers. Towards those he disliked he could be forbidding, and the late Clifford K. Shipton recalled on one occasion being ejected from the Society for simply rubbing Librarian Bates the wrong way; but he could also be charming. Mary Helen Kidder, who assisted him for eight years in the 1930s, has said of him that "one would not guess that underneath so stern an exterior there lurks a keen sense of humor." A fine judge of character, his recollections of some of the characters who frequented the Historical Society reveal an unexpected quality of tolerance as well as an eye for eccentric detail.

In his position as Librarian and Recording Secretary, Albert Bates served under seven Presidents of the Society. His relationships with members and officers were sometimes strained, but he was always civil: John Stedman, President from 1890 to 1894, struck Bates as a man only mildly interested in the affairs of the Society; towards Dr. Hoadly, President from 1894 to 1900, Albert Bates had great respect; his relationship with the Reverend Samuel Hart, President from 1900 to 1917, was unquestionably serene, and President Hart frequently underscored in his own reports the points Bates made in his. In his autobiographical notes, Bates is silent about Hart's successors, but in his correspondence and annual reports he made fairly clear his displeasure with the modest salary paid him by the Society, his need for a trained assistant, and his dissatisfaction with the reluctance of the institution, following the large bequest of George E. Hoadley in 1923, to build a new home for itself. There were inevitable disagreements, but his loyalty, clearly, was to the institution and to the cause of Connecticut history.

In his Librarian's report for 1922, Albert Bates reviewed the accomplishments of his 30 years of service in the "Historical Rooms" at the Atheneum. In 1892, he noted, funds were "exceedingly limited and the prestige of the Society had become somewhat dimmed through the death of members and general lack of interest," but there were already signs of a revival of interest in 1890 when Bates arrived and, by 1922, the condition of the institution had been vastly improved. Membership had doubled, the annual income had increased five-

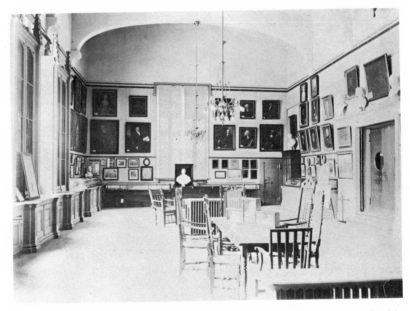

One of the two "historical rooms" of the Society in the Atheneum building, the Museum photographed in January, 1895

. 69 .

The Library of the Society photographed in December, 1894

fold, and the size of the collections had multiplied. Without book cataloging to guide him, Bates could not specify the actual number of books and manuscripts added to the Library, so he indicated growth by approximating expanded shelf space: "the genealogies occupy more than five times their former space, the local histories at least four times what they did, newspapers require perhaps eight to ten times their former shelf space, manuscripts have grown to four or five times their former number." With the assistance of an annual State grant of $1,000 which began in 1893, 17 volumes of the *Collections* had been published. Interest in the Society was clearly growing and monthly meetings were well attended.

There was also, Bates suggested, a darker side. The Society had picked up a room for its newspapers underneath the stairs of the Morgan Memorial building at the Atheneum, but the shift required the Librarian to climb a steep staircase bearing heavy bound volumes. The most serious problem was the lack of open shelf space for additional books acquired for the Library. Growth demanded space, declared Bates, and without free shelves there was no way to perform the relatively simple task of organizing and classifying materials for the collections. It was evident that the pressing need for an assistant had not been answered, nor were there funds to begin the cataloging of the collections.

In the following 18 years, his last as active Librarian of the Society, some of these problems were nevertheless overcome. Bates's salary was increased in 1930, and the first full-time assistant was hired in 1928. In 1934 a modest four page quarterly, the *Bulletin* of The Connecticut Historical Society, commenced publication. Through the generosity of members, prompted no doubt by Albert Bates's grim recitals of the institution's needs, the financial state of affairs improved steadily. After George E. Hoadley's death in 1923, it was discovered that this quiet businessman, Charles J. Hoadly's brother, had left the Society over $250,000 for the purpose of constructing a fireproof building. At first officers were reluctant to give up the guaranteed space at the Atheneum, but the argument for a new building eventually proved convincing and, in 1929, a parcel of land on the corner of Hartford's Washington and Buckingham Streets was purchased.

When the market value of many investments of the Society fell during the Depression, the decision to build on the new site had to be postponed. It was a bitter disappointment to Albert Bates that he could not convince the officers to proceed and have an appropriate structure erected, but, happily, he lived past the day when, in 1950, the Society purchased the home of Curtis Veeder and converted it to house and display its collections. Although Bates had opposed its purchase, he insisted on being led through the building by Thompson R. Harlow, his successor. Since he had become nearly blind, everything had to be described to him, but his skepticism was overcome and, according to Harlow, "he was so delighted that he presented his splendid collection of Indian relics and arranged for the gift of his 2,400 volume collection of early juveniles."

Albert Bates always found pleasure in the joys of collecting. The pursuit and discovery, the negotiations and the savoring of the occasional triumph drew upon his varied skills as an historian and bibliographer as well as on his instincts as a businessman. Most of what he purchased was for the Society, though he frequently had to buy items out of his own pocket and secure payment later on. He also put together large and valuable personal collections of stamps, coins, Indian relics, and American juveniles which he began acquiring in the 1890s, well before children's books became so generally prized, explaining, "their quaintness and illustrations intrigued me." These small books with their paper covers and woodcut illustrations must have appealed to his interest in printing, his sense of humor and, because they were not yet "collectable," to his pocket book. One day, Bates later recalled, he was called to New Haven by a dealer to examine the contents of a store, closed up for 25 years, but once owned by the Babcock family, perhaps the most successful publishers of children's books in the State. He returned to Hartford with his collection enlarged by 600 titles, to which he later added numerous editions of the *New England Primer* and the *History of Holy Jesus,* a number of Isaiah Thomas imprints, several "battledores," and even an English horn book.

In 1953, a year before his death, Albert Bates donated his priceless collection of American juveniles to The Connecticut Historical Society where they are currently kept in a large secretary built by Aaron Chapin for Thomas Robbins. His collection thus joined the 3,500 children's books left to the Society in 1927 by Caroline M. Hewins, Hartford's pioneer in the development of library services for the young. As a consequence of these two magnificent gifts, the holdings of the Historical Society in the field of children's literature now rank among the four largest in the United States. The Society continues to build upon this collection by acquiring, whenever possible, early juveniles printed in Connecticut.

What Albert Bates called the "revival" of the Society stemmed, in part, from the fervent interest in genealogy that spread through certain levels of American society in the late nineteenth century. This was a period when immigration from southern and eastern Europe was altering the character of many New England towns and cities. It was also a time when

An English "horn book" from the collection of juveniles donated by Albert Carlos Bates to The Connecticut Historical Society

political power was shifting in many areas to those who could effectively represent or lead the new American voters. Of the various responses to this shift in the character of the population, the most important to the development of The Connecticut Historical Society was the organization of patriotic and hereditary associations. Americans began to join such organizations in increasing numbers, prompted, according to Samuel Eliot Morison, by a "reflex desire for distinction in a country of growing uniformity, a human craving for fellowship among the urban masses who missed their old village and neighborhood associations." In contrast to the less exclusive Elks and Knights of Columbus, the hereditary societies such as the Sons and Daughters of the American Revolution, the Colonial Dames, and the Society of Mayflower Descendants were based on race and ancestry and were, to Morison, "essentially a drawing together of the older American stock against their polyglot competitors."

As admission to these societies required proof of ancestry, ambitious applicants turned out in increasing numbers to establish their lines of descent. An upsurge in readers at the Historical Society in 1893 led Albert Bates, himself a Son of the American Revolution, to wonder whether it was only a "popular craze" or a more long-lasting interest. If it were to continue, he informed members, "the books most used must soon be replaced by new copies." The interest persisted and the Society did its best to meet the needs of what Bates called the "genealogical workers." As Librarian he pressed for additional funds to purchase the D. Williams Patterson Library which added 800 volumes and 1,100 pamphlets to the collections. Each subsequent year family histories have been added so that today, The Connecticut Historical Society, with its printed genealogies and town histories located in the Reading Room, shares with the State Library the distinction of possessing the most extensive genealogical collection in the State. As an additional service to members, the Historical Society has made available, since 1950, a loan collection of town histories and genealogies. Known as the Charles G. Woodward Loan Collection in honor of the donor of the original core of loan books, it was supplemented in 1956 by a deposit of the Society of Mayflower Descendants in the State of Connecticut.

In 1938, as he was approaching his 46th year as Librarian, Albert Bates's health began to fail. Because his assistant, Mary Helen Kidder, had become engaged and was preparing to leave the Society, it became imperative to find a replacement. A search began with the expectation that the new assistant, after a sufficient demonstration of ability, would probably succeed Bates as Librarian. Less than two years after Thompson R. Harlow, a graduate of the University of North Carolina, was hired, Albert Bates wrote to Edgar F. Waterman, President, resigning his position of Librarian and suggesting that Thompson Harlow succeed him following the annual meeting. In May, 1940 Thompson Harlow became the Society's sixth Librarian, and Albert Bates was named Librarian Emeritus, remaining Recording Secretary until 1943 when the office was passed first to Harlow and then to Miss Frances A. Hoxie.

It has been one of the special qualities of The Connecticut

Historical Society that it has valued equally the participation and interest of antiquarian and genealogist, academic and lay historian, old Yankee and recent citizen. Samuel Eliot Morison recalls that as a graduate student at Harvard he was refused the privilege of examining the card catalog of the Massachusetts Historical Society. He would not have been so treated at The Connecticut Historical Society for, in the era of Albert Carlos Bates, access to the books was granted to a wide range of readers and use of the manuscripts, though more restrictive, was generally permitted to legitimate scholars and Ph.D. candidates upon written application to the Standing Committee. Limits have been eased since then, and use of the collections is open to all adults with a genuine interest in Connecticut history who will observe the necessary precautions for their care. The achievements of Albert Bates have been noted, but it should be emphasized that he also did much to assure the balanced role taken by the Historical Society. He served the needs of genealogists hoping they would take the "short step . . . to a study of the history of the places and times in which their ancestors lived." He was also as useful as he could be to professional historians like Charles McLean Andrews at Yale and George M. Dutcher at Wesleyan, both members of the Society. Among other rare book librarians like Lawrence C. Wroth and Clarence S. Brigham, he was a much valued friend and colleague. With Albert Bates as its Librarian, The Connecticut Historical Society learned that it could be both popular and professional.

The Recent Past
1940–1975

THE INSTALLATION OF A NEW Librarian in May of 1940 marks the beginning of the most successful as well as the most recent chapter in the life of The Connecticut Historical Society. It was not evident at the time, but the next 35 years have proved to be enormously productive ones, embracing a period when much of the original promise of the institution, and perhaps a bit more, has been realized. Under the leadership of Thompson R. Harlow, Director, the Historical Society has been transformed from a small library-museum run by three people on a modest budget into a complex and professional organization staffed by 15 with an annual budget 20 times what it was in 1940. Much of the credit belongs to Thompson Harlow who brought to his post a number of valuable qualities: a working knowledge of library practice, a sympathy for the many and varied tasks he would be called upon to perform, and a gift for personal relationships that was to insure an ever widening circle of involvement by members in the affairs of the Society. When the Standing Committee in 1938 began its search for an Assistant Librarian, it was decided that what was needed was a scholar rather than an administrator; in fact, the committee filled the position with a man who has served equally well in both capacities.

As Albert Bates's yearly May reports made clear, the condition of the institution in the late 1930s did not give much cause for comfort. The budget would not permit an expansion of staff; there were inadequate funds for the purchase of books and almost no money for museum acquisitions; and, the library and manuscript collections were inadequately cataloged. Perhaps half the Society's books were included in an author catalog, but without location symbols. Retrieving a book or a manuscript required either a photographic memory or perfect intuition. On the prosaic level of maintenance, the Society did not own a vacuum cleaner. The museum collections were also generally uncataloged, imperfectly labeled, and improperly stored. Museum displays consisted of densely packed glass cases filled with miscellaneous relics, with chips of the Plymouth Rock and pieces of the Charter Oak, competing for attention with far more important objects. Through patient and intelligent collecting, the Society had become the repository of invaluable materials, yet much of that collection was without value to researchers simply because it was impossible to identify and retrieve.

As his first annual reports make clear, Thompson Harlow understood perfectly the dimensions of the task ahead. In 1940 he warned the membership against "actually living in the past":

> The Society is badly cramped for adequate space, not only for display purposes, but for proper shelving of our manuscripts and books. The catalogue is entirely inadequate for the use of the Society. Every object in the library should be so recorded that any attendant can immediately locate it. Collections of manuscripts should be analyzed for materials on other people and subjects. Our membership is decreasing since each year we lose more through resignations and deaths than we admit in new members.

Albert Bates had delivered similar jeremiads in previous years to little avail, but the response in 1941 indicated that the concern with efficiency and future growth was broadly shared among the members. At a regular meeting in April, 1941, Richard M. G. Potter, one of the younger members, recommended that a committee be formed to consider ways of improving the operations of the institution. In his recital of the Society's difficulties, Potter stressed the same problems that had been identified in the previous decades: crowded quarters, lack of shelf space, inaccessibility of the collections, difficulties of displaying museum objects in limited quarters, the static membership roll, and the reluctance of potential donors to turn valuable objects over to the Society. What Potter hoped was that the Committee, formed by unanimous vote at that meeting, might be able to identify courses of action that would lead the Society out of the doldrums.

The Committee together with Thompson Harlow presented a set of guidelines on future acquisitions to the membership at the next annual meeting in May, 1941. For the first time since 1839 an explicit list of priorities was set down on paper to inform the members of the goals of the Society and to direct future purchases. Connecticut imprints, newspapers, and monographs on State history were foremost among the desiderata, while scrap books, manuscripts relating to Connecticut, and the published records of institutions within the State stood on the next level of importance, followed by maps, engravings, paintings and items of furniture executed by Connecticut artists and craftsmen. The resolution was unanimously adopted and an Acquisitions Committee was formed, a decision which demonstrated the useful participation of members in shaping the future direction of the institution. In one sense, the priorities established in 1941 have stood up fairly well over the course of time. Whether it be books, manuscripts, scrap books, portraits or pieces of furniture, the principle of selection demands that the object under consideration have a close association with Connecticut. The Historical Society is vitally concerned with the products of Connecticut authors and printers, painters and craftsmen, and with all sources reflecting the character of life within the State. With such a clear policy it has been possible to build a strong and useful collection on a limited budget.

The guidelines adopted in 1941, however, suggest a much stronger emphasis on the development of the Library than on the Museum, but that policy reflected the orientation to the past, the still pervasive influence of Albert Bates, and possibly the view of the young Thompson Harlow. It was not long before the two spheres of activity, the Library and the Museum, were given equal weight and emphasis. Ten years later Thompson Harlow was called to account by one member for neglecting the Library in favor of the Museum. It was a case of deceptive appearances, for while the Museum had come far in the previous decade, the collection of books, pamphlets and manuscripts had been given equal attention. In the year when the remark was made, in fact, "more was spent on acquisitions for the library than in the previous years since 1825." What surprised and delighted many members was the facility with which the Society's Librarian acquired a thorough knowledge of American painting and furniture, and there is no more fitting comment on the results of that education than the one offered in 1963 by Newton Case Brainard, then President of the Society:

> He came to us a fledgling Librarian. His interest in that field has never flagged and fellow librarians have more than once commented on his wide and accurate knowledge.
>
> He has never overlooked the fact that as an historical society we must not ignore pertinent subjects which are outside of the library. Today he is at home with the experts on American furniture as well as those on American art. He is familiar with the multitude of objects of daily life in the colonial days which are important in appraising our history.

In turn, Thompson Harlow's growing familiarity with the fine and decorative arts of Connecticut was made possible by his ability to work closely with such eminent collectors and experts as Newton C. Brainard, George Dudley Seymour, Philip H. Hammerslough, Penrose R. Hoopes, and Frederick K. Barbour.

The more aggressive program for the development of the Society was inevitably postponed by the onset of war. In August, 1943, Thompson Harlow was inducted into the army and granted an indefinite leave from the Society. Miss Frances A. Hoxie, who was hired as a Library Assistant in 1939, became Acting Librarian in his place and she bravely kept up reader's services, despite the reduction of staff to one person. In his

The Library of the Society, with Miss Frances A. Hoxie at her desk, photographed in the Winter of 1942–1943

first two-and-a-half years as the Society's Librarian, Thompson Harlow had achieved much. Several exhibitions, one fittingly enough on war relics, were organized. Energetic members discovered that their interest in the running of the Society was fully welcomed and needed. At the same time, Harlow gradually prepared the membership to think in terms of a much increased staff. In his *Annual Report* in 1943, he divided his activities into three categories, that of librarian, curator, and editor, each of which, he added, "could readily be a full-time post." In the capacity of Librarian, he admitted his failure to find funds for a part-time cataloger, but patiently explained what progress had been made in that department and what benefits could be expected in the future. Systematically cataloging the manuscript holdings would bring to light, he assured his audience, untold treasures as well as insure the more effective use of the collections. In his report on the museum, he described changes in acquisitions procedures and hinted briefly at the first results of the more active program of seeking out important and appropriate collections for the So-

George Dudley Seymour (1859–1945), Vice-President of the Society, 1933–1945, attributed to John Henry Niemeyer

ciety. The *Annual Report* of 1943 thus provided the Society with its first optimistic assessment in many years.

It was not until December, 1945 that Thompson Harlow was able to return to his position as Librarian. Severely wounded in Europe, he was forced to spend 18 months recuperating before recovering his health. Meanwhile the collections had been significantly increased through the impressive bequest of George Dudley Seymour (1859–1945) of New Haven, which consisted of a large collection of early American furniture, portraits, glass and pottery and included a handsome sum of money to assist in its care and display. It was the first significant *collection* of museum objects to be donated to the Society and represented the first fruits of the new policy enunciated by Thompson Harlow.

Appreciation of the distinctiveness of Connecticut furniture has been a recent development, and the Seymour Collection, consisting largely of Connecticut pieces, has played a role in furthering that interest. A successful patent lawyer, George Dudley Seymour devoted much of his private life to various historical causes. He was an accomplished genealogist and historian, a member of a number of patriotic and historical societies, and an untiring student of the life of Nathan Hale. In 1914 he purchased the birthplace of Hale in South Coventry, supervised its restoration and eventually willed the old home to The Antiquarian & Landmarks Society, of Connecticut, Inc. With a love of Connecticut history that was engrained from boyhood, Seymour began associating with Hartford antique collectors and dealers as early as his high school days. After his return to Connecticut in 1883, he acquired family pieces which had been carefully passed on through the generations. From dealers and various "pickers" and directly from farm porches and attics, he purchased many pieces "in the rough" to augment his collection. Most of his purchases were made in Hartford and New Haven counties and carried with them tales of origins and ownership which Seymour carefully recorded.

George Dudley Seymour was also a member, from 1918, of the Walpole Society, a select coterie of connoisseurs formed in 1910 to share good company and a common love of the products of early American craftsmen. Recognition of the beauty and strengths of American design in the decorative arts was then a relatively new discovery and informed collecting in this area had only really begun in the years immediately following the first Centennial of the nation. The Walpole Society brought together a number of New England pioneers in the collecting and study of American antiques, several of whom were also members of the Historical Society. Connecticut was well represented in the Walpole Society, and the first dinner of the original Walpolians took place at Heublein's Hotel in Hartford. In time, the Historical Society was to be the beneficiary of the connoisseurship of several members of this organization, particularly George Dudley Seymour, Newton Case Brainard, and Morgan Bulkeley Brainard. In January of 1950, Thompson Harlow organized an exhibition of some of the Society's most prized possessions for one of the Walpole Society's semi-annual gatherings, which proved an appropriate tribute to an influential group of collectors as well as a striking record of the Society's own achievements in the field.

The gift of George Dudley Seymour's collection to the Society literally doubled the museum holdings, but nearly all of it had to remain in storage because of lack of space for its display, and those who doubted the need for a new building were now converted. In 1946 the Society briefly considered, but soon rejected, the idea of sharing a building with the Hartford Public Library and the Watkinson Library. The cost of construction, together with the projected overhead expenses, delayed any immediate solution to the pressing need for more space. There were important signs of progress on other fronts, however: attendance at monthly meetings, membership level and accessions returned to and then surpassed pre-war levels; the publication of the *Bulletin* was resumed and a grant from the Hartford Foundation for Public Giving in 1947 permitted the Society to employ an experienced cataloger to begin a thorough dictionary catalog of the Society's books and pamphlets together with an imprint catalog of books published in the State up to 1876. By 1949 it could be announced that "more and more, reliance can be placed on the catalogue and its value is being displayed daily." The restoration of painting and furniture, which had begun in the 1930s on the initiative of George D. Seymour, was now given new emphasis through the informed guidance of Newton C. Brainard, an increasingly important figure in the affairs of the Society.

The real turning point in the development of the Society occurred in 1950 with the purchase and subsequent remodeling of the residence of Curtis H. Veeder located at 1 Elizabeth Street in Hartford. The acquisition of the Veeder property was the fortunate conclusion to a hurried search for a new building that commenced in February, 1950, following a ruling of the Fire Marshal of the City of Hartford which threatened to virtually close the Society's doors. Located ten minutes from the center of Hartford, with sufficient acreage to permit generous parking and future expansion, the fire-resistant Veeder building was reasonable enough in price to permit the Society to invest all that would be needed to convert it to its needs while releasing the income from the still substantial

Newton Case Brainard (1880–1964), President of the Society, 1953–1963, painted by Martin Kellogg in 1963

building fund for operating expenses. The purchase of the property was completed on June 23, 1950 and the move commenced on the 26th. The departure from Main Street ended a close working relationship with the Watkinson Library and marked the completion of the Society's years at the Atheneum. Acquisition of the building, declared Thompson Harlow at the March, 1950 meeting, "marks the beginning of an era during which the Society will take its proper place in the life of Hartford and the State of Connecticut, and when its entire function of collecting, preserving and disseminating the history of Connecticut is finally possible."

The succeeding 25 years, from 1950 to 1975, have seen this prediction largely fulfilled. The financial condition of the Society, upon which all services must depend, has steadily improved. Total endowment as of April 30, 1974, in book value, reached $4,458,038 which in turn, together with dues and trusts yielded an income of $272,350. The growth of the endowment can be attributed to the generosity of numerous members and to the successful management of the Society's funds. Compared to the income at the beginning of the century, or even in 1940, the increase is truly impressive. The continued growth of income has permitted the addition of much needed staff, an increase in publications, and a dramatic expansion of the acquisitions budget. The financial position of The Connecticut Historical Society compared to the historical societies of Vermont, New Hampshire, Maine and Rhode Island is distinctly favorable, but in comparison with the large budgets of the State funded institutions of the Mid-West and West, the level of spending is actually quite modest. Much can be achieved within the present budget, but any major increase in service must be supported, as in the past, by additional private contributions and foundation grants.

It was apparent at the time of purchase that the new home of the Society would require modification and several additions before it could house the collections and provide needed space for all activities. The first alteration in the original structure was the addition of a bookstack which was completed in 1951. Profits from investments enabled the Historical Society to proceed in 1956, after a delay caused by the devastating flood of the previous year, with the construction of the Hoadley Auditorium, named in honor of one of the Society's most generous benefactors. Completed in Fall, 1956, the auditorium provided the Society with a large meeting hall, display walls for the unique collection of tavern signs given by Morgan B. Brainard, and storage space in the basement below. The need for additional display areas in order to exhibit the important collection of Connecticut furniture from Frederick K. and Margaret R. Barbour and the need for a storage area to house manuscripts hampered efficient operations until the erection in 1971 of a large well-designed addition. The new wing provided museum exhibition areas, additional storage space, a new reading room and manuscript "stack" space, as well as modern offices. For the first time in the institution's history, there is sufficient room, at least for the moment, for all activities and collections under one roof.

One of Thompson Harlow's original goals was the addition

Frederick K. Barbour (1894–1971), donor, together with his wife, Margaret R. Barbour, of the "Barbour Collection" of Connecticut furniture. Painting by Raymond P. R. Neilson, 1954

of well-qualified specialists to assume in various areas the burden of work that was carried, almost exclusively in 1940, by the Librarian. Ever since Thomas Robbins became "the man of the Society" in 1844, the Librarian was also expected to perform the duties of curator. From the arrival of Albert Bates, the Librarian had also come to assume the functions of an editor. To perform these tasks, Albert Bates and, at the beginning of his tenure, Thompson Harlow, could only rely on one additional staff member. In 1947 a cataloger was added, and in 1949 a genealogist joined the staff as "Chief of the Reading Room." In successive years, the staff was enlarge by the addition of an editor, a curator, a curator of prints, a manuscript cataloger, a registrar and a photographer. The capacity of the Society to respond to the many queries that are sent in daily has been increased many fold. The unaccessioned and uncataloged material will, in time, be brought under control, and the number and variety of exhibitions that can be mounted in a given space of time has been significantly increased.

Perhaps the most important development of the last 35 years has been the evolution of a well-balanced historical society in which barriers between library and museum have broken down and the collections, in the full range of media, have been studied with important scholarly consequences. When Walter Muir Whitehill surveyed the field of private historical societies in 1960, he found few words of praise for those institutions that had not followed the example of Massachu-

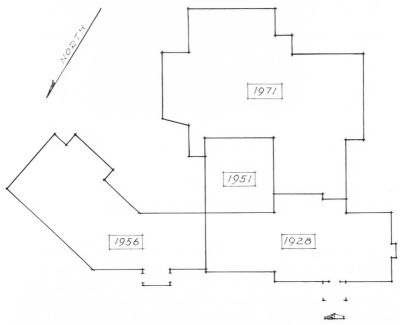

Diagram showing the expansion of The Connecticut Historical Society at its present One Elizabeth Street home. The section, 1928, is the original Curtis Veeder house which includes partial basement, two floors, and an attic, totalling an area of 16,000 square feet. A three-floor Bookstack was added, 1951, 5,500 square feet; an Auditorium, 1956, with basement and one floor, 10,600 square feet; and the new wing, 1971, containing offices, Museum, Reading Room, and partial basement in a three-story structure, 31,000 square feet. The whole of the present facility makes 63,000 square feet available for services to the public

Thompson R. Harlow, Director of The Connecticut Historical Society

setts in abandoning their museum collections entirely. Since
the addition of a curatorial staff and with the more systematic
cataloging of manuscript and print holdings, the intercon-
nections between the two spheres of activity are becoming
closer every day. Genealogies permit the Society to trace the
lines of descent through which museum objects have passed,
and manuscript holdings have revealed new pieces of information about obscure Connecticut craftsmen. The best demonstration of the interdependence of the two departments are
the annual painting exhibitions held each year, with a few
exceptions, since 1954. In most cases, the exhibition and catalog draws equally from the Society's print, manuscript, and
museum holdings to present a comprehensive picture of an
important Connecticut artist. The Society's resources, developed over a 150 year period, will continue to offer to the re-
searcher and student in every field of Connecticut history the
materials on which future histories will be based.

In the years since the Historical Society was founded in

1825, the number of research libraries and museums within Connecticut has steadily grown. The field, once occupied by only a few institutions, has now become rather densely populated, but the position of The Connecticut Historical Society remains secure and its future assured because it has identified as its goal the collection and preservation of historical materials related strictly to Connecticut history. The judgment of countless individuals and the concession from other institutions that something "belongs" at the Historical Society bears witness to a successful past and a hopeful future.